INTRODUCTION

In the course of that portion of World War II in which the USA was an active combatant — a period of less than four years — the Army Air Forces played a significant role in all operational theatres. Boeing B-17 bombers and Curtiss P-40 fighters were among the aircraft caught on the ground in Hawaii and destroyed in large numbers by the first Japanese attack in December 1941; and Boeing B-29s of the AAF were responsible for dropping the atom bombs over Hiroshima and Nagasaki that spelt the end of the war for Japan. In the intervening years, a massive effort against the Axis powers was mounted by the Air Forces based in Europe, spearheaded by the Combined Bomber Offensive shared by the Eighth Air Force and the Royal Air Force.

Under the impetus of such operational necessity, the pace of aeronautical development in all the combatant nations accelerated dramatically, but nowhere as fast, perhaps, as in the USA. For many years, that great nation had been isolated both by geography and by politics from the realities of military aircraft development in other lands and in consequence the Army Air Forces in 1941 were technically ill-equipped to wage a major air war. Already, however, some lessons were being learned from the experiences of France, Britain and other European nations that had put US-designed aircraft (principally fighters) into action. A start had already been made, for instance, to increase the armament and armour protection of Army fighters then in service, and to design and build new types of very much greater performance.

Until the beginning of the 'forties, AAF dogma had placed emphasis upon the strategic bomber; little attention had been given to the development in the USA of the true defensive fighter, such types as the Bell P-39 and Curtiss P-40 being compromised by the requirement that they should have a good low-altitude ground-attack performance, for use in coastal defence around the USA. Although both these types were produced in large numbers and the P-40, indeed, remained in production until 1944, a whole new generation of fighters had to emerge before the USAAF could meet its opponents on equal — and eventually, superior — terms.

This volume is one of two in the Fact File series devoted to US Army fighters of World War II; the division is alphabetical by manufacturer, with the Bell and Curtiss types included in this volume and the Lockheed, North American and Republic types, with others, in the second part. As it happens, this division is largely a chronological one also, for the major entries in this first part are concerned with the initial generation of World War II fighters while the greatly superior second generation — the Lightning, the Mustang and the Thunderbolt — appear in the second volume. By the time the war ended, however, a third generation was emerging — the jet fighter generation — and among the 13 types of fighter included in this Fact File will be found three of these jet fighters, including the Bell P-59, the only American jet type to reach operational (but not combat) service before the end of the war. Comparison between these jet types and such fighters as the Curtiss P-36 and Bell P-39 clearly indicates just how much progress occurred in those few years of wartime effort.

Curtiss P-40s, more than any other type of fighter operated by the US Army Air Forces during World War II, were decorated with distinctive nose insignia, of which the Shark's Teeth of General Claire Chennault's "Flying Tigers" became the most famous. Illustrated here is the somewhat stylized Bengal Tiger's head adopted by the 11th Fighter Squadron (342nd Fighter Group) which was commanded by Chennault's son, Major John Chennault, and operated P-40Es from primitive airstrips in Alaska.

BELL P-39 AIRACOBRA

Fighter aircraft development in the USA in the mid-'thirties was strongly influenced by the then-current doctrine of the Army Air Corps that assumed "the ascendancy of bombardment over pursuit aircraft". While this line of thought eventually brought into service such effective bombers as the Boeing B-17 and Consolidated B-24, it led to the neglect of first-class fighter design, since the main requirements for such aircraft were conceived to be coastal defence and army close support. Geographically and politically, the USA appeared to be isolated from the threat of bombing attacks, and little thought was given to the development of true interceptors with day and night capability of the European style.

When the perils of pursuing this doctrine began to emerge towards the end of the decade, rapid and effective action was taken by the US aircraft industry and the Army Air Corps to produce efficient fighting aircraft such as the P-51, P-47 and later versions of the P-38 (all of which are described in Part Two of this work). In the meantime, however, the effects of this policy were well shown by the emergence of the Bell P-39, a fighter of mixed qualities that never achieved the more sanguine of its backers expectations and that proved a near disaster in some of its operational deployments, yet achieved considerable success in certain roles. In the official history of the USAAF in World War II the P-39 is described as "especially disappointing" with "a low ceiling, slow rate of climb and relative lack of manoeuvrability [which] put its pilots at a decided disadvantage wherever they fought". On the other hand, the Airacobra repeatedly showed its worth in low-level strafing and bombing and, as General Kenney reported from the SW Pacific, it could

"slug it out, absorb gunfire and fly home". Pilots assigned to fly the P-39 enjoyed its flying qualities if not its fighting performance, but experienced frustrating equipment failures that added up to a poor serviceability record. Despite the shortcomings that became evident soon after the P-39 entered service, a total of 9,585 Airacobras was built, and of these almost exactly half, 4,773, were supplied to the Soviet Union, where they enjoyed a good reputation in the ground support role.

The P-39 was the second fighter design of the Bell Aircraft Corporation (and, indeed, the company's second aircraft of *any* type to be built), work on which had begun soon after the company was founded in 1935. Its founder, Lawrence D Bell, had been vice-president of the Consolidated company until the latter moved from Buffalo, NY, to California; Bell then started his own company in the Buffalo factory with 56 employees and a sub-contract to make wing components for Consolidated PBY flying boats. A US Army Air Corps contract was obtained by Bell to build a prototype (and, later, a service test quantity) of an unconventional twin-engined fighter, the XFM-1 Airacuda, with pusher engines and gunners in nacelles on the wings.

A similar willingness to break with convention was demonstrated by Bell's senior engineers — Robert J

(Below) The Bell XP-39, prototype of the Airacobra series, as first flown with air intakes for the carburettor and turbosupercharger on the fuselage sides. (Above right) The prototype after modification to XP-39B with dorsal and wing root intakes.

(Above) A service test YP-39, showing the nose armament installation. (Below) The P-39C was the initial production standard for the Airacobra, soon superseded by the P-39D.

Woods and Harland M Poyer — in the design of their second Air Corps fighter, conceived during 1936. The design team had been particularly impressed by the potential of the 37-mm Oldsmobile cannon demonstrated by the American Armament Corporation during 1935 and evolved a layout for a single seat fighter that allowed such a weapon to be located in the nose on the aircraft's centreline, for maximum accuracy and ease of installation. This in turn led to the idea of locating the engine amidships close to the centre of gravity, with a long extension-shaft to drive the propeller and the cannon firing through the spinner. In the early design studies the pilot was located well aft, virtually in the base of the fin, to obtain the best weight

Early evolution of the Airacobra is depicted in these side views of (1), the XP-39; (2), the XP-39B and (3), the P-39C with enlarged vertical tail; the P-39D featured a small dorsal fin fillet and a belly rack, shown by dotted line.

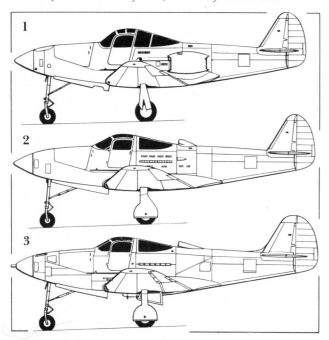

distribution, but this proved unsatisfactory in terms of forward view and the cockpit was finally located just ahead of the engine. The concentration of weight about the CG gave the fighter excellent manoeuvrability but, as many pilots would eventually discover to their cost, made it extremely susceptible to small changes of CG position, such as occurred, for example, when the ammunition for the cannon was expended.

The central engine location left space available in the front fuselage to stow a nosewheel so a tricycle undercarriage was adopted as another of the Bell fighter's unconventional features. Two 0.30-in (7,7-mm) machine guns were added to the nose-mounted cannon to make the design one of the most heavily armed single-seaters of its day, and many advanced features of structural engineering were also adopted. Details of the Bell proposal were submitted to the Army Air Corps in a specification dated 18 May 1937 and this submission won a contract for a single prototype, to be designated XP-39 and ordered on 7 October 1937. Bell proposed, at this stage, to use the Allison V-1710-17 engine, rated at 1,150 hp and fitted with B-5 turbo-supercharger on the port side of the centre fuselage; large air intakes were fitted each side of the fuselage, one supplying air to the turbo-supercharger and the other to the Prestone cooler and the carburettor. Additional intakes, for oil cooling air, were located in the wing roots. The propeller reduction gear was located well forward in the nose, so the long extension shaft from the engine, passing close beneath the pilot's seat, turned at full crankshaft rpm. As an alternative to the 37-mm cannon, Bell considered installing a 25-mm weapon in the nose, but the prototype XP-39 was in fact unarmed for its first flight, which was made at Wright Field, Ohio, on 6 April 1938 by Jimmy Taylor, a free-lance test pilot of great experience.

Flying at a relatively light weight without armament, the XP-39 demonstrated an excellent rate of climb, reaching 20,000 ft (6 100 m) in five minutes, and achieved a maximum speed of 390 mph (628 km/h) at that altitude. Even had it been fully laden, this prototype would have weighed only 6,204 lb (2 817 kg), whereas service versions would be flying at 8,200 lb (3 720 kg) with no compensating increase in engine power, and therein lay one of the Airacobra's short-comings. However, the prototype's performance, ease of handling, and generally advanced concept impressed the Army Air Corps in 1938 sufficiently for a service test batch to be ordered, comprising 13 YP-39s. While these were under construction, the XP-39 test results and characteristics were analysed by the NACA, and the Army requested Bell to make a number of modifications suggested by NACA to improve the aircraft's general performance and its suitability for low-altitude close-support operations in which the Army remained principally interested. These changes included removing the turbo-supercharger and the fuselage-side air intakes; installing an Allison V-1710-39 engine that delivered 1,090 hp at its rated altitude of 13,300 ft (4 055 m), thus restricting the aircraft's high-altitude performance; locating a carburettor air intake on top of the engine bay just aft of the fuselage and ducting air from the port wing root intake to the Prestone cooler; lowering the top line of the cabin and making changes to the undercarriage. Wing span was decreased from 35 ft 10 in (10,92 m) to 34 ft (10,37 m) and overall length was increased from 28 ft 8 in (8,74 m) to 29 ft 9 in (9,07 m).

Redesignated XP-39B, the prototype resumed flight trials on 25 November 1939, the gross weight now being 6,450 lb (2 930 kg). Because of the power plant changes, the XP-39B now took 7.5 minutes to reach 20,000 ft (6 100 m) and the top speed at 15,000 ft (4 575 m) decreased to 375 mph (603 km/h); however, manoeuvrability at low altitudes was enhanced and the Air Corps was satisfied that the modifications were worth while, and in January 1940 directed Bell to complete the YP-39s without turbo-superchargers.

First flown on 13 September 1940, the first of the service-test YP-39s (Bell Model 12) was generally similar to the XP-39B but had a V-1710-37 engine and the full armament of one 37-mm cannon (with 15 rounds) in the nose plus the pair of 0.50-in (12,7-mm) machine guns (200 rpg) and an additional 0.30-in (7,62-mm) gun with 500 rounds, also in the nose. The size of the fin and rudder was increased (this modification later being applied to the XP-39B and adopted as standard for the production aircraft) and the addition of some armour protection for the pilot brought the gross weight to 7,235 lb (3 285 kg). The designation XP-39A covered the proposed installation of a 1,150 hp V-1710-31 engine with high altitude rating, in one of the service test aircraft, but the installation was not made.

Just three weeks and three days before the start of World War II, the Army Air Corps placed its first production contract for the Bell fighter, ordering 80 aircraft to a similar standard as the YP-39 and to be designated P-45, although this was soon changed to P-39C (Bell Model 13). Deliveries began in January 1941, but by then a contract change had called for installation of self-sealing fuel tanks and a further increase in armament, with four wing-mounted 0.30-in (7,62-mm) guns (1,000 rpg) replacing the two of this calibre in the nose. Provision was also made for a 500-lb (227-kg) bomb or a 75-US gal (289-l) drop tank to be carried in this new version, designated the P-39D (Bell Model 15), and only 20 P-39Cs were built.

Additional contracts eventually brought the total of P-39Ds delivered to 923, including the balance of 60 on the original order, but before these began to reach the USAAF (as the Army Air Corps became at the end of 1941) Bell was delivering a similar model to Britain for use by the Royal Air Force. An order had been placed on 13 April 1940 by the British Direct Purchase Commission in Washington for no fewer than 675 Bell Model 14s, although no flight assessment was made of the type by a British pilot until eight months after this order had been placed, Bell's claims of a top speed in excess of 400 mph (644 km/h), operating altitude of more than 36,000 ft (10 973 m) and cruising range of over 1,000 mls (1 610 km) apparently having been taken at their face value. They were based, in fact, upon performance tests with a highly polished prototype flying at a weight some 2,200 lb (1 000 kg) lower than that at which the RAF Airacobras would enter service, as Bell eventually admitted.

The British version of the Bell fighter, for which the name Caribou was initially chosen, but then dropped in favour of retaining the official American name, was substantially the same as the P-39D with the exception that a 20-mm Hispano M1 cannon was substituted for the 37-mm weapon, with 60 rounds; the engine was the 1,150 hp Allison V-1710-E4, an export version of the -35. Deliveries began from the Bell plant in May 1941 but because shipment had to be made by sea, the first Airacobra was not assembled and ready to fly in Britain until 6 July; this particular aircraft was, in fact, one of three P-39Cs supplied under the terms of the Lend-Lease Act, preceding the first British-purchased Model

A Bell P-39D Airacobra (identified by the dorsal fin fillet, wing machine guns and belly bomb racks), in 1941, carrying the markings of the 39th Squadron, 31st Pursuit Group.

(Above) The Bell P-39F, shown here with the red-bordered US star insignia that was used only from July to September 1943, differed from the P-39D only in having an Aeroproducts propeller. (Below) A Bell P-39D-2, with Curtiss propeller.

(Below) One of the three XP-39E development aircraft, showing the revised tail unit; plans for installation of a Continental IV-1430-1 engine in this version did not materialize.

14s by a week or two, but by the end of September, 11 Airacobra Is had been supplied to No 601 "County of London" Squadron, R Aux AF, which had been chosen as the first to equip with the new fighter, under Sqdn Ldr E J Gracie, DFC. After a brief training period at Matlaske, Norfolk, No 601 moved to Duxford, Cambs, for operations.

During trials by the Air Fighting Development Unit at Duxford, the performance of the Airacobra proved disappointing, the max speed being 33 mph (53 km/h) lower than anticipated. Although pleasant to fly, the Bell fighter was found to be definitely inferior to the Hurricane and Spitfire in rate of climb and ceiling, whilst its 750-yd (686-m) take-off run precluded its use from some of the smaller fighter fields then being used by the RAF. Armament accessibility was extremely poor, and there was a lethal concentration of carbon monoxide in the cockpit after the nose machine guns had been fired; moreover, the firing of these guns almost invariably rendered the compass useless, this being rated by the RAF as the most serious impediment to the operational debut of the type.

After the introduction of a number of modifications, the Airacobra I was finally cleared for trial operations by No 601 Squadron, for which four aircraft were moved forward to RAF Manston. Four missions were flown over the French coast and some invasion barges were strafed but the aircraft were pulled back to Duxford on 11 October. Lack of spares and the need for further modifications contributed to an extremely high unserviceability rate; no further operations were undertaken and the Airacobra was withdrawn from RAF service in December. A batch of 150 P-39Ds earmarked for Lend-Lease delivery as Airacobra IAs did not materialize.

Of the 675 Model 14s ordered by Britain, 212 were diverted to the Soviet Union and 54 were lost at sea during delivery. Another 179 were taken over by the USAAF in December 1941 immediately following the attack on Pearl Harbor, for emergency use in the South Pacific. These repossessed British aircraft received the designation P-400 and retained RAF serial numbers with American markings; more than 100, together with 90 P-39Ds, were despatched to Australia between 23 December 1941 and 18 March 1942 to reinforce Army units already based in the Pacific area, including the 15th Fighter Group, which had P-39s serving with the 46th Fighter Squadron on Hawaii at the time of the Japanese attack. The P-39Ds had begun to reach Army Air Corps Squadrons in the USA earlier in 1941, the first to equip being the 31st Pursuit Group (comprising the 39th, 40th and 41st Pursuit Squadrons), followed by the 58th Pursuit Group with the 67th, 68th and 69th Pursuit Squadrons. Before departing for combat, the three squadrons of the 31st PG were reassigned to the 35th Fighter Group for service with the 5th Air Force (all unit designations had changed from Pursuit to Fighter in this period).

In the fast-changing situation in the South Pacific in the early months of 1942, P-39 units were rushed into action piecemeal, both pilots and ground crews suffering extreme discomfort from the local conditions as well as from a lack of regular supplies, and, of course, enemy action. A typical case was that of the 67th Fighter Squadron, which was assigned to the defence of the French island of New Caledonia, where its personnel disembarked on 15 March 1942. Three pilots had trained with the unit since September 1940 and were therefore "veterans"; 18 others fresh from flying school had joined the squadron a few weeks before embarkation, seven had joined at Brooklyn as the unit sailed and another 15 had been added in Australia, where they were flying P-40s. The equipment comprised 45 P-400s and two P-39Ds, which arrived in crates; the only available airfield was still under construction at Tontouta, 35 mls (56 km) from the harbour. Only one truck and trailer was available to transport the crated aircraft, which were moved at the rate of three every 24 hours without interruption for 16 days.

Arrived at Tontouta, the ground personnel found there were no handbooks of any kind for the P-400, although there were instructions for later P-39 variants. There were no spares and every fifth aircraft was therefore assigned for use as spares; assembly called for improvisation of a high order and was undertaken in the open, often in heavy rain and with the minimum of tools. Nevertheless, the 67th's first P-400 flew at Tontouta on 28 March 1942 and thereafter the aircraft were completed at the rate of one a day.

The P-400s and P-39Ds of the 35th Group's 40th and 41st Fighter Squadrons moved up to Port Moresby from Australia in May 1942 and were quickly in combat. The deficiencies of the Airacobra soon became apparent — notably, the 37-mm gun gave endless trouble, continually jamming when fired, and the poor rate of climb meant that many Japanese raids came in unopposed. The official AAF history was to record, after the war ended, that "The Airacobra even in a good state of repair, was unable to meet the Japanese fighters on equal terms". However, individual pilots achieved considerable successes with the type — the 40th & 41st Fighter Squadrons, for example, recorded two instances of Zero-Sens being hit head-on by 37-mm cannon fire and disintegrating completely, while the entire tail assembly of a twin-engined bomber was similarly blown off. The 20-mm cannon in the P-400s, although reliable, did not prove so popular with pilots, who preferred the 0.50-in (12,7-mm) machine guns because of their greater ammunition capacity. The Airacobra's fighting effectiveness was enhanced with the introduction of the P-38 into the area, as the Lockheed fighters were able to meet the Japanese attackers at higher altitudes and force them down to levels where the nimble P-39s and P-400s could out-manoeuvre them.

In the dive-bombing role, P-39s achieved a good success rate, their pilots often adopting a vertical dive to launch the bomb at 2,000 ft (610 m) before pulling out. To supplement the single bomb on the centreline, a

The P-39Q, final production version of the Airacobra, was built primarily for supply to the Soviet Union. New features were the 0.50-in (12.7-mm) machine guns carried in underwing fairings, plus some internal changes.

Bell P-39D Airacobra Cutaway Drawing Key

1 Aluminium sheet rudder tip
2 Rudder upper hinge
3 Aerial attachment
4 Fin forward spar
5 Tail navigation lights
6 Fin structure
7 Rudder middle hinge
8 Rudder
9 Rudder tab
10 Rudder tab flexible shaft
11 Elevator control quadrant
12 Rudder control quadrant
13 Starboard elevator
14 Starboard tailplane
15 Rudder lower hinge
16 Control cables
17 Fuselage aft frame
18 Diagonal brace
19 Fin root fillet
20 Elevator hinge fairing
21 Elevator tab (port only)
22 Port elevator
23 Aerial

24 Aerial mast
25 Port tailplane
26 Aft fuselage semi-
   monocoque structure
27 Radio installation
28 Access panel
29 Radio equipment tray
30 Control quadrant
31 Oil tank armour plate
32 Aft fuselage/central chassis
   bulkhead
33 Engine oil tank
34 Prestone (cooler) expansion
   tank
35 Carburettor intake fairing
36 Carburettor intake shutter
   housing
37 Engine accessories
38 Central chassis web
39 Frame
40 Starboard longitudinal
   fuselage beam
41 Exhaust stubs
42 Allison V-1710-35 Vee 12-
   cylinder engine
43 Engine compartment
   decking
44 Aft-vision glazing
45 Crash turnover bulkhead
46 Turnover bulkhead armour
   plate
47 Auxiliary air intake

61 Aileron servo tab
62 Wing rib
63 Starboard navigation light
64 Ammunition tanks
65 Two 0.3-in (7,62-mm) wing
   machine guns
66 Inboard gun ammunition
   feed chute
67 Machine gun barrels
68 Mainwheel door fairing
69 Starboard mainwheel
70 Axle
71 Mainwheel fork
72 Torque links
73 Mainwheel oleo leg
74 Wing fuel cells (6)
75 Fuel filler cap
76 Mainwheel retraction
   spindle
77 Fuel tank gauge capacity
   plate
78 Fuel tank access plate
79 Forward main spar
80 Oil cooler intakes

96 Instrument panel frame
97 Control column
98 Control column yoke/drive
   shaft
99 Nosewheel retraction chain
   coupling
100 Rudder pedal assembly
101 Fuselage machine gun
   ammunition tank

110 Cannon aft support frame
111 37-mm M4 cannon breech
112 Circular endless belt-type
   cannon magazine (30
   rounds)
113 Cockpit forward armoured
   plate
114 Two 0.5-in (12,7-mm)
   fuselage machine guns
115 Flap links
116 Aileron tab actuating link
117 Aileron control
118 Aileron trim tab
119 Aileron servo tab
120 Wing skinning

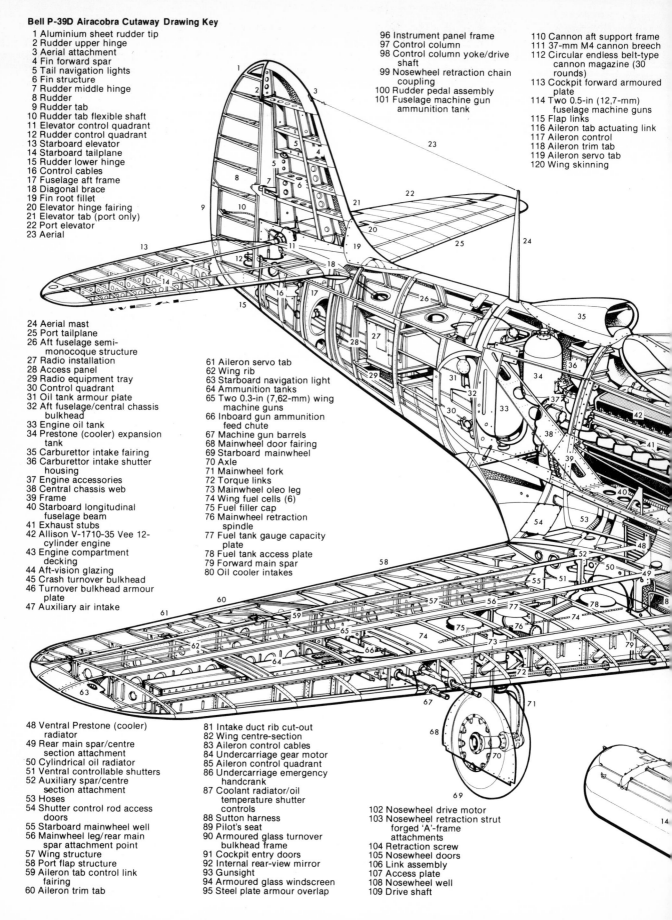

48 Ventral Prestone (cooler)
   radiator
49 Rear main spar/centre
   section attachment
50 Cylindrical oil radiator
51 Ventral controllable shutters
52 Auxiliary spar/centre
   section attachment
53 Hoses
54 Shutter control rod access
   doors
55 Starboard mainwheel well
56 Mainwheel leg/rear main
   spar attachment point
57 Wing structure
58 Port flap structure
59 Aileron tab control link
   fairing
60 Aileron trim tab

81 Intake duct rib cut-out
82 Wing centre-section
83 Aileron control cables
84 Undercarriage gear motor
85 Aileron control quadrant
86 Undercarriage emergency
   handcrank
87 Coolant radiator/oil
   temperature shutter
   controls
88 Sutton harness
89 Pilot's seat
90 Armoured glass turnover
   bulkhead frame
91 Cockpit entry doors
92 Internal rear-view mirror
93 Gunsight
94 Armoured glass windscreen
95 Steel plate armour overlap

102 Nosewheel drive motor
103 Nosewheel retraction strut
   forged 'A'-frame
   attachments
104 Retraction screw
105 Nosewheel doors
106 Link assembly
107 Access plate
108 Nosewheel well
109 Drive shaft

field modification was devised to allow P-39s to carry one 100-lb (45,4-kg) or 300-lb (136-kg) bomb under each wing in lieu of the inboard wing machine guns; this allowed the drop tank to be carried for longer range missions, but the heavier bombs were found to have an adverse effect on the ailerons. A favourite weapon devised by the squadrons of the 35th FG for dive bombing attacks comprised the 75-US gal (289-l) drop tank filled, in equal parts, with engine oil and 100-octane petrol, and with three incendiary bombs strapped beneath. This weapon proved extremely effective against wooden bridges, buildings and cocoanut palm revetments, targets fired in this way often being reported as still burning the following day.

In an attempt to improve the rate of climb of the P-400s and P-39s, some units reduced the amount of ammunition carried to 500 rpg for the four wing guns and 45 rounds for the 20-mm cannon. Bell also advised, during 1942, the steps that could be taken in the field to reduce the combat weight of the P-39 by about 1,000 lb (454 kg) and a few aircraft were so modified, with greatly improved low-altitude manoeuvrability and rate of climb. Other local modifications investigated included fitting four 0.50-in (12,7-mm) guns in place of the smaller calibre weapons in the wings, and testing a 200 US gal (757-l) drop tank, both these innovations being made in early 1943. Shortage of spares remained a constant problem, however, and ground crews performed near-miracles of improvisation to keep their aircraft flying, often using parts from one variant to repair another. An extreme example of this process was provided by a P-400 serving with the 68th Fighter Squadron, which ended up flying in combat with one P-39D wing, one P-39K wing and a V-1710-63 engine.

Alongside the 35th and 58th Fighter Groups, already mentioned, the 8th Fighter Group (made up of the 35th, 36th and 80th Fighter Squadrons) also flew P-39s in the Pacific from September 1942 onwards. Initial combat service was interrupted, however, in February 1943 when the Group's personnel was so decimated by the effects of malaria that the unit had to be withdrawn to Australia, returning to the combat theatre in April and

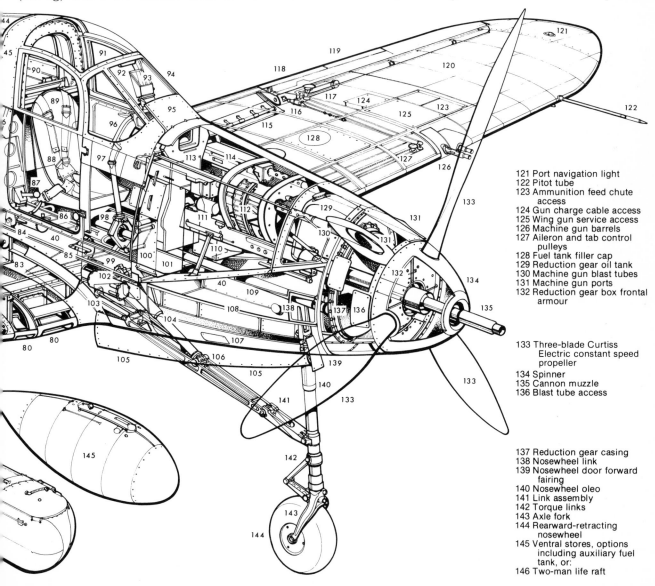

121 Port navigation light
122 Pitot tube
123 Ammunition feed chute access
124 Gun charge cable access
125 Wing gun service access
126 Machine gun barrels
127 Aileron and tab control pulleys
128 Fuel tank filler cap
129 Reduction gear oil tank
130 Machine gun blast tubes
131 Machine gun ports
132 Reduction gear box frontal armour

133 Three-blade Curtiss Electric constant speed propeller
134 Spinner
135 Cannon muzzle
136 Blast tube access

137 Reduction gear casing
138 Nosewheel link
139 Nosewheel door forward fairing
140 Nosewheel oleo
141 Link assembly
142 Torque links
143 Axle fork
144 Rearward-retracting nosewheel
145 Ventral stores, options including auxiliary fuel tank, or:
146 Two-man life raft

then serving in the Pacific until the end of the war, retaining its P-39s until 1944.

While the Airacobra had been receiving its combat initiation in the hands of the RAF and the Army Air Force in the Pacific, production had been continuing on P-39D variants ordered with Lend-Lease funds for supply to the Soviet Union. These comprised 336 P-39D-1s with 20-mm M1 cannon in place of the 37-mm M4 weapon, and incorporating a small dorsal fin fillet that became a standard feature of all subsequent variants, and 158 P-39D-2s that introduced the 1,325 hp V-1710-63 engine. Like the British Airacobras, these batches became subject to repossession by the AAF to meet pressing operational needs in 1942, and a few went to the Pacific area alongside the P-400s previously

The three-view drawing below depicts the P-39Q version of the Airacobra; the additional side-view (bottom) shows the TP-39 trainer.

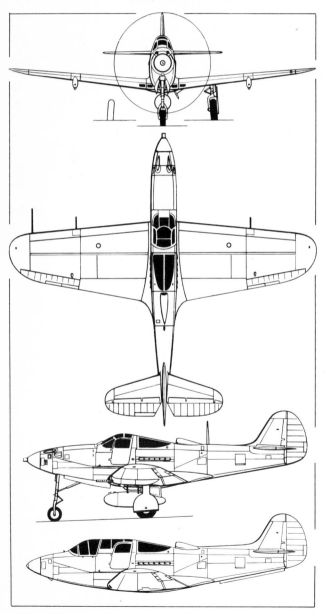

mentioned, while others were used — also with P-400s — to help equip units of the US 12th Air Force when it was formed in the Middle East in the autumn of 1942. Two P-39 Fighter Groups — the 81st and the 350th — were assigned to the theatre at the end of 1942 as part of the American contribution to the Operation Torch landings in North Africa. The ground echelons of the 81st arriving in French Morocco in November and the air echelons flying in from the UK between December 1942 and February 1943 after a period of training in England. The 81st FG, comprising the 91st, 92nd and 93rd Fighter Squadrons, began combat operations with the 12th AF in January 1943 and the 350th FG's squadrons, comprising the 345th, 346th and 347th, began operations at about the same time. Their task was to support the ground operations in the Allied drive against Asian forces in Tunisia, for which they flew primarily in a low-altitude close-support role, often escorted by Spitfires and P-40s of other 12th AF Fighter Groups. Also flying P-39s in North Africa on tactical reconnaissance and close support duties was one squadron, the 154th, of the 68th Observation Group, but this began to re-equip with the F-6A Mustang in April 1943.

The 81st and 350th Fighter Groups retained their P-39s until 1944. The former provided protection for Allied shipping in the Mediterranean after the Tunisian campaign ended and covered convoys landing troops in Sicily during July. It then supported the landings at Anzio in January 1944 before moving to India and re-equipping with P-40s. The 350th FG moved up with the Allied advance in Italy, retaining its P-39s until the autumn of 1944 when it converted to P-47s, having first won a Distinguished Unit Citation for an action with its P-39s on 6 April 1944 when the Group flew 10 missions in the face of intense flak and attacks by numerous enemy interceptors to hit troops, bridges, vehicles, barracks and air warning installations.

By the time these P-39-equipped Groups reached Italy they had relinquished the P-400s and were flying a mix of later production models of the Airacobra. Some of the P-39Ds had been converted to P-39D-3 and D-4 for ground attack duties, having armoured oil and glycol coolers and two cameras in the rear fuselage. Also by the end of 1942, Airacobras had gone into service, somewhat fortuitously, with two other air forces. The first of these was the Royal Australian Air Force which, on 27 July 1942, received the first 14 of an eventual total of 22 Airacobras, including both P-39D and P-39F variants respectively with 20-mm and 37-mm cannon; five more were handed over to the RAAF in May and three in June 1943. The initial batch of 14 was operated variously by Nos 23, 24, 82 and 83 Squadrons, RAAF, as emergency reinforcements at a time when the invasion of Australia by Japanese forces appeared to be imminent. As this threat receded, the Airacobras were withdrawn and returned to the USAAF, together with those delivered in 1943 which had remained in storage, and by November 1943 none remained in the RAAF inventory. The Portuguese *Arma da Aeronautica* had meanwhile acquired a total of 18 P-39s that had made forced landings while flying from England to North Africa in December and January 1942 to equip the 81st Fighter Groups; initially interned, these aircraft were subsequently purchased (together with a single P-38) and served in Portugal for several years.

When the decision to adopt an Aeroproducts constant-speed hydraulic propeller was taken in 1942, replacing the Curtiss Electric unit used previously, the designations P-39F and P-39G were assigned to aircraft having the same characteristics, in other respects, as the P-39D-1 and P-39D-2. They could be distinguished externally by the use of twelve exhaust stubs fitted on each side of the engine bay, instead of the normal six. The use of "dash numbers" to indicate small improvements introduced in each successive production block had not been adopted at the time these Airacobra variants entered production; consequently, new suffix letters had to be adopted for each development stage and the number of variants appeared to proliferate, although there were only small changes involved.

Orders were placed for 254 P-39Fs and 1,800 P-39Gs, but the last 25 of the former type were completed with V-1710-59 engines and were consequently designated P-39Js. Of the 229 P-39Fs actually built, some were modified at Field Modification Centres to have the extra armour and cameras for ground attack and tactical reconnaissance duties, then becoming P-39F-2s. None of the P-39Gs (Bell Model 26) on order actually materialized in this guise: the first 210 emerged as P-39K-1s, these being virtually the same as the P-39G as ordered, with V-1710-63 engine and Aeroproducts

This Bell P-39Q-5 was converted to an unarmed training version of the Airacobra with a second cockpit added ahead of the first, and a small, long ventral fin.

propeller. Then followed 250 P-39Ls, which differed from the K in reverting to the Curtiss propeller. Compared with the P-39D, the L model also had an increased gross weight, up to 9,100 lb (4 131 kg) instead of 8,850 lb (4 018 kg), with a normal combat weight of 7,900 lb (3 587 kg) compared with 7,650 lb (3 473 kg).

Another engine change, to the V-1710-83 with Curtiss Electric propeller, changed the designation to P-39M for the next 240 aircraft. This engine had a take-off rating of only 1,200 hp compared with 1,325 for the V-1710-63, and the take-off performance of the P-39M suffered accordingly. However, the output was improved at high altitudes and the P-39M had a top speed, for example, of 370 mph (595 km/h) at 15,000 ft (4 575 m), compared with the P-39L's 360 mph (579 km/h) at the same altitude and weight. This speed,

Bell P-39D Specification

Power Plant: One Allison V-1710-35 12-cylinder liquid-cooled Vee engine with single-stage supercharger, rated at 1,150 hp for take-off at sea level and at military power at 12,000 ft (3 660 m) and with a continuous rating of 1,000 hp at 10,800 ft (3 294 m). Curtiss Electric constant speed three-bladed propeller of 10 ft 5 in (3,18 m) diameter. Fuel capacity, 120 US gal (454 l) in 12 wing tanks; provision for one 75 US gal (284 l), 156 US gal (500 l) or 175 US gal (662 l) drop tank under fuselage.
Performance (at 7,650 lb/3 473 kg weight): Max speeds, 335 mph (539 km/h) at 5,000 ft (1 525 m), 360 mph (579 km/h) at 15,000 ft (4 575 m) and 324 mph (521 km/h) at 25,000 ft (7 625 m); rate of climb, 2,550 ft/min (12,9 m/sec) at 5,000 ft (1 525 m); time to climb to 10,000 ft (3 050 m), 3.9 min, to 20,000 ft (6 100 m), 9.1 min, to 25,000 ft (7 625 m), 14.0 min; take-off distance to 50 ft (15,2 m), 2,600 ft (793 m); range at max cruise power, 350 mls (563 km) at 10,000 ft (3 050 m); max range, with drop tank, 1,100 mls (1 770 km) at 10,000 ft (3 050 m).
Weights: Basic equipped, 6,300 lb (2 860 kg); normal combat, 7,650 lb (3 473 kg); max take-off, 8,850 lb (4 018 kg).
Dimensions: Span, 34 ft 0 in (10,37 m); length, 30 ft 2 in (9,21 m); height, 11 ft 10 in (3,60 m) undercarriage track, 11 ft 4 in (3,46 m); wheelbase, 11 ft 9¾ in (3,60 m); wing area, 213 sq ft (19,79 m²); dihedral 5 deg 36 min constant.
Armament: One 37-mm M4 cannon with 30 rounds and two 0.50-in (12,7-mm) Colt-Browning machine guns with 200 rpg in fuselage nose; two 0.30-in (7,62-mm) machine guns in each wing with 1,000 rpg. Provision for one bomb of up to 500-lb (227-kg) weight under fuselage.

Bell P-39N Specification

Power Plant: One Allison V-1710-85 12-cylinder liquid-cooled Vee engine with single-stage supercharger, rated at 1,200 hp for take-off at sea level, 1,125 hp military rating at 15,500 ft (4 728 m) and 1,000 hp continuous at 14,000 ft (4 270 m). Aeroproducts constant speed three-bladed propeller of 11 ft 7 in (3,53-m) diameter. Fuel capacity, 87 US gal (329 l) in eight wing tanks; provision for one 75 US gal (284 l), 156 US gal (590 l) or 175 US gal (662 l) drop tank under fuselage.
Performance (at 7,600-lb/³ 450-kg weight): Max speeds, 330 mph (531 km/h) at 5,000 ft (1 525 m), 376 mph (605 km/h) at 15,00 ft (4 575 m) and 368 mph (592 km/h) at 25,000 ft (7 625 m); rate of climb, 2,600 ft/min (13,2 m/sec) at 5,000 ft (1 525 m); time to climb to 5,000 ft (1 525 m), 2 min, to 15,000 ft (4 575 m), 6.1 min to 25,000 ft (7 625 m) 11.9 min; take-off distance to 50 ft (15,2 m), 2,550 ft (778 m); range at max cruise power, 300 mls (483 km) at 10,000 ft (3 050 m); max range with drop tank, 975 mls (1 570 km).
Weights: Basic equipped, 6,400 lb (2 906 kg); normal combat, 7,600 lb (3 450 kg); max take-off, 8,800 lb (3 995 kg).
Dimensions: Span, 34 ft 0 in (10,37 m); length, 30 ft 2 in (9,21 m); height, 12 ft 5 in (3,79 m); undercarriage track, 11 ft 4 in (3,46 m); wing area, 213 sq ft (19,79 m²); dihedral, 5 deg 36 min constant.
Armament: One 37-mm M4 cannon with 30 rounds and two 0.50-in (12,7-mm) Colt-Browning machine guns with 200 rpg in fuselage nose; two 0.30-in (7,62-mm) machine guns in each wing with 1,000 rpg. Provision for one bomb of up to 500-lb (227-kg) weight under fuselage.

in 1943, was still too low to make the P-39 a good fighter at medium to high altitudes, however, and it remained essentially a low-altitude ground support aeroplane in all its versions.

The last production variants, P-39N and P-39Q, were the most-produced Airacobra models and were built primarily for Lend-Lease supply to the Soviet Union. The P-39N, of which 2,095 examples were built, had the V-1710-85 engine, with the same rated output as the P-39M's -83 engine but driving an Aeroproducts propeller of 11 ft 7 in (5,53-m) diameter, 14 in (35,6-cm) larger than any previous Airacobra propeller. The first 166 P-39Ns were built with the standard fuel capacity of 120 US gal (462 l) in 12 wing tanks, but later aircraft had four tanks deleted to reduce the capacity to 87 US gal (335 l) in order to restrict the weight to 8,800 lb (3 990 kg); kits were made available, however, for all later P-39Ns to be converted to have the full original capacity. The final 695 N models were P-39N-5s with SCR-695 radio in place of SCR-535A, reduced weight of aarmour and a curved armour head plate supplementing the bullet-proof glass behind the pilot.

(Above) A British Airacobra I repossessed by the USAAF and operated as a P-400, with a mixture of British and American markings, to train RAAF pilots at Laverton, Australia, early in 1942.

Production of the P-39Q totalled 4,905, this designation indicating a change of armament from four 0.30-in (7,62-mm) to two 0.50-in (12,7-mm) machine guns in the wings, the two guns of the latter calibre being retained in the nose with the 37-mm M4 cannon. The wing guns were carried in fairings under the wings, but in the P-39Q-20 and subsequent, they were dispensed with altogether, and some of these later batches also used a four-bladed Aeroproducts propeller of 11 ft 7 in (3,53-m) diameter. A three-bladed propeller of 11 ft (3,36-m) diameter was also tried, in the P-39Q-30, but most of the Q models used the larger diameter three-bladed unit. Like the later P-39Ns, the P-39Qs were built initially with the eight-tank wings, but the P-39Q-5 had ten tanks and a capacity of 110 US gal (424 l) and in the P-39Q-10 and subsequent blocks the full wing capacity was restored.

Although most of the P-39Qs went to Russia, 75 were assigned to the 332nd Fighter Group, which took them to Italy to serve with the 15th Air Force in February 1944, but retained them for only a few months before receiving P-47s. Use of the Airacobras by this Group's 100th, 301st and 302nd Fighter Squadrons, plus the Italian operation by the 350th FG already described, effectively brought to an end the Airacobra's operational use by the USAAF, although it served in the Soviet Union until the end of the war. A few examples were converted to two-seat trainers with a second cockpit ahead of the first, beneath a lengthened canopy; the first such example was designated TP-39F and a few others were known as RP-39Qs. A radio-controlled target version of the Airacobra, investigated with the designation A-7, did not proceed.

As well as the combat operation with Fighter Groups attached to the 12th and 5th Air Forces in the Mediterranean and Pacific theatres, the P-39 saw service with USAAF units stationed in many other parts of the world, these including the 15th Fighter Group, which was serving as part of the defence force for the Hawaiian Islands at the time of the Japanese attack on Pearl Harbor, and one of the squadrons of which (the 46th Fighter Squadron) had P-39s in service at that time. After the 18th Fighter Group had moved to the South Pacific in March 1943 to join the 13th Air Force, this unit also flew P-39s, together with other types, operationally. Airacobras flew with the 54th Fighter Group in Alaska, the 342nd Composite Group in

(Above left and below) Bell P-39Ds and P-39Fs were used by the RAAF for a short time in 1943, being operated by No 23 Squadron in whose markings these examples are shown.

(Above) The Airacobra I only ever equipped one RAF squadron, this being No 601, and it proved unsuitable for combat without much effort, which could not be spared in 1941.

Iceland and the 32nd, 36th and 53rd Fighter Groups in the Panama Canal Zone.

Between 1941 and 1944, when the P-39 was in production, it was subject to relatively little design development, but three early P-39Ds were modified to flight test the experimental Continental V-1430-1 engine and were then designated XP-39E. New features of this variant, apart from the engine, were a laminar-flow wing with square-cut tips and each of the three aircraft tested had different vertical tail surfaces, the first being conical, the second cut-off square and being rather short and the third being square-cut also but taller. The dorsal carburettor air intake was relocated farther back along the fuselage and the wing root radiator intakes were enlarged. Wing span and area were increased to 35 ft 10 in (10,92 m) and 236 sq ft (21,92 m) respectively and empty and loaded weights were 6,936 lb (3 150 kg) and 8,918 lb (4 050 kg) respectively. The Continental engine was not, in fact, fitted in the XP-39Es, which flew, starting in February 1942, with the Allison V-1710-47, achieving a speed of 386 mph (621 km/h) at 21,680 ft (6 608 m). An order for 4,000 P-76 production examples of the P-39E was placed with the Bell Marietta factory but was cancelled three months later and the type remained wholly experimental; however, the work done by Bell on these aircraft was put to use in development of the P-63 Kingcobra (see page 21).

Apart from the major use of P-39s made by the USAAF and Soviet Air Force and its small-scale use by the RAF, RAAF and Portuguese Air Force, two other services operated the type during World War II, these being the Free French Air Force and the Italian Co-Belligerent Air Force. A total of 165 P-39Ns and P-39Qs

(Above) An early production Airacobra I for the RAF, before delivery, with non-standard rudder and (below) one of three Lend-Lease P-39Ds that preceded the Airacobra Is to Britain.

was supplied to the *Forces Aeriennes Francaises Libres* for service in North Africa, starting in May 1943, and these aircraft first equipped GC III/6 *Rousillon* at Ain-Sefra. Next month, GC I/5 *Champagne* and GC I/4 *Navarre* equipped on P-39Ns at Medouina, these three squadrons making up the *3e escadre*, which was assigned to serve with Coastal Command in Algeria. While engaged in these operations, Lt Le Gloan, the

From May 1943 onwards, the Forces Aériennes Francaises Libres *(Free French Air Force) received 165 P-39Ns and P-39Qs for service in North Africa.*

its P-39s into northern Italy in support of Allied operations, where it was subsequently followed by the *5e escadre.*

Italian operation of P-39Qs followed the capitulation on 8 September 1943 and the subsequent creation of the Italian Co-Belligerent Air Force from units of the *Regia Aeronautica* wishing to take up arms against Germany. A miscellany of about 200 Italian aircraft came over to the Allies but were mostly unsuitable for combat use, and the Allies agreed, on 24 May 1944, to make new aircraft available to the Co-Belligerent Air Force. These "new" aircraft in the event comprised used Spitfires and P-39s that had become surplus to requirements in Italy (plus some Martin Baltimore light bombers). The Airacobras comprised 75 P-39Qs and 74 P-39Ns, drawn from 15th Air Force stocks at Naples.

Training of Italian crews drawn from the 12° *gruppo* (4° *stormo*) began at Campo Vesuvio in June 1944, with personnel of the 9° and 10° *gruppi* (also 4° *stormo*) following in July, and the first squadrons to form on the P-39Q, the 73a and 91a *squadriglia*, equipped on the type at Leverano (Lecce) on 11 September 1944. These units transferred to Galatina (Lecce) in October, where they were joined in due course by the 96a and 97a *squadriglia* of the 9° *grupo* and the 84a and 90a *squadriglia* of the 10° *grupo.*

Italian-crewed P-39 operations began on 18 September 1944 with sorties over the Albanian front and continued at a low rate until the end of the year, entirely in the Mediterranean and Balkan theatres. A few losses occurred as close support and ground attack operations continued into 1945, the Co-Belligerent Air Force Airacobra squadrons flying also from Cannes, where the 10° and 12° *gruppi* had 89 P-39s in service in May 1945; others were also operated by the *Scuola Addestramento Bombardamento e Caccia.*

leading French fighter ace with 18 confirmed victories, and in command of the 5e *Escadrille* of GC III/6, was killed on 11 September 1943.

P-39Qs became available to the Free French forces in 1944, allowing additional units to equip on the type — GG III/3 *Ardennes*, GC II/6 *Travail* and II/9 *Auvergne*, forming the *5e escadre.* The GC I/3 *Corse* also equipped on P-39Ns in 1943, and GC I/9 *Limousin* received P-39Qs in February 1945. The 3e *escadre* took

Like the Free French Air Force, the Italian Co-Belligerent Air Force received examples of the P-39N and P-39Q from USAAF stocks in Europe, operating them alongside the Allied air forces from September 1944 until the end of the war.

BELL P-59 AIRACOMET

By the time World War II ended, three of the principal combatants — Germany, Britain and the USA — had jet propelled fighters at various stages of initial operational deployment, and designers in many countries were already directing almost all their talents towards the future application of this radical form of propulsion to aircraft of all categories. The gas turbine, as a prime mover, was one of the most important advances in the aeronautical state of the art to emerge in the war-time period, and the speed with which it was developed in the three aforesaid nations was indicative of the high priority that jet propulsion enjoyed — despite initial official reluctance, especially in Britain, to sponsor the work. Nevertheless, it was the British work, based on the pioneering designs of Wg Cdr Frank Whittle, that allowed the USAAF to initiate the development, during 1941, of what would be its first turbojet-powered aircraft, and the first Allied fighter to fly that was designed from the outset to use this form of propulsion.

The initiative that led to the design and production of this aircraft by Bell Aircraft Corp was taken directly by Major General Henry H Arnold as Chief of the Army Air Force. In April 1941, he had witnessed Whittle engines under test in England and had seen the prototype Gloster-Whittle E.28/39 (Britain's first jet aeroplane) a few weeks prior to its first flight. Returning to the USA in May, Gen Arnold put in hand negotiations that led to America acquiring rights for General Electric to build and develop the Whittle-designed turbojet. On 4 September 1941, at a meeting of USAAF and GE representatives held at Wright Field, the decision was taken to proceed with construction of 15 engines and three airframes, and Bell was chosen to design the latter. This decision was communicated to Bell (represented by Larry Bell and his chief engineer Harland M Poyer) next day; until that moment, Bell was wholly ignorant of the availability of jet engines and had given no prior consideration to the design of a suitable aircraft to make use of such propulsion. Nevertheless, the company immediately agreed to tackle the task and accepted an extremely tight schedule that called for completion of the first prototype eight months from signing of the contract, which actually took place on 30 September 1941.

Bell had been chosen for this historic task for several reasons, among which were the facts that it was rather less overloaded with work on other fighters than were other manufacturers with fighter experience, that it was close to General Electric's facilities, that it had a small but highly respected and imaginative engineering staff plus the driving enthusiasm of Larry Bell himself for research and development of all kinds, and finally that it had some isolated facilities that would make it easier to preserve secrecy. From the outset, a very high degree of secrecy was specified; this was reflected not only in the various measures taken to maintain security at the design and engineering buildings involved — such as

(Above and below) Air and ground views of the Bell XP-59A in its initial test configuration as the first jet aircraft built and flown in the USA.

welding windows shut — but also in the use of the XP-59A designation for the prototypes, when the XP-59 was a totally different (Bell) design for a twin-boom fighter with piston engine driving a pusher propeller, work on which was quietly discontinued. Anyone coming across references to the XP-59A would therefore assume it was a version of the earlier fighter. The contract document itself referred simply to "twin-engine, single place interceptor pursuit models" and as a further concession to secrecy, no allocation of the usual USAAF serial numbers was made until after the prototypes had flown, the numbers eventually being in sequence with those of the pre-production batch of XP-59As. Even when the YP-59A prototypes had been completed, they were frequently fitted with dummy propellers and canvas covers when being moved from one location to another.

Despite a lack of fully detailed design and performance data on the engine, which was designated the Type I-A by General Electric in the first instance, Bell engineers worked quickly to establish the overall configuration of the XP-59A, which acquired the company designation of Model 27. Although the primary purpose of the aircraft was to investigate jet propulsion, it was also to be designed to be suitable for use as a fighter, provided that no unforeseen snags arose with the power plant. The configuration chosen was a straightforward mid-wing monoplane of relatively low aspect ratio, with engines fitted in nacelles beneath the wing roots and flush against the sides of the fuselage. The flush-riveted light-alloy skinned wing comprised

Another in-flight view of the original XP-59A, showing the large wing area, small jetpipe and relatively slender fuselage. As part of the overall security precautions, serial numbers were not allocated to the prototypes until after flight testing had begun.

inner and outer panels and had two spars plus an auxiliary third spar in the inner panels, to which the main legs of the tricycle, electrically-actuated, undercarriage were attached. The fuselage consisted of two main sections, the forward section having two built-up longitudinal beams with transverse bulkhead frames and stringers to reinforce the outer skin, and the aft section being a stressed-skin monocoque. All control surfaces were fabric covered and manually operated; fabric-covered flaps were electrically operated.

Pressurization and heating of the cockpit was by means of air bleed from each engine compressor and hot exhaust air was used to de-ice the cockpit canopies; access, in the XP-59As, was through a side-hinged canopy. Specified armament (fitted in the second and third prototypes) consisted of two 37-mm M4 cannon in the nose with 44 rpg. Fuel was carried in self-sealing

tanks in the wings, the total capacity being only 290 US gal (1 097 l).

Construction of the first XP-59A began early in January 1942 in a factory Bell had leased from the Ford Motor Co in Buffalo, NY, and after some delays caused by slippage in the engine delivery schedule, this airframe — packed in crates — was shipped out on 12 September 1942. Travelling by rail, it took seven days to reach Muroc, California, where a suitable test site had been selected in the Rogers Dry Lake, close to the USAAF Bombing and Gunnery Range — a site that would eventually blossom out as the Edwards AFB. There, on 1 October 1942, Bell's chief test pilot Robert Stanley made a tentative first flight, with undercarriage down and at a maximum height of 25 ft (7,6 m). Three more flights were made that day, at altitudes up to 100 ft (31 m), followed by four more on 2 October, one by a USAAF pilot, in which a maximum altitude of 10,000 ft (3 050 m) was reached. This record of eight flights in two days speaks well for the reliability of the I-A engines, but these were, inevitably, the source of considerable trouble in the early days of testing and the XP-59A soon became known, unofficially, as "Miss Fire".

The ninth flight was not made until 30 October. By

(Above left) While being ground-handled at the desert air base where Airacomet testing was located, the XP-59A prototype was crudely camouflaged with a dummy propeller. (Below) A radio-controlled P-59B (furthest from camera) and the final YP-59A modified as a drone controller, with extra cockpit in the nose.

(Above and below right) The P-59A was the production version of the Airacomet, built only in small numbers and used to equip the USAAF's first jet fighter squadrons in 1945.

that date, the XP-59A had received some necessary modifications to the undercarriage, and had also been fitted with a rudimentary seat for a flight test observer in the armament bay ahead of the cockpit, with a hole in the upper decking and a small windscreen. Engine problems, including malfunctioning fuel pumps, overheated bearings, detached turbine blades and a tendency to "flame-out", slowed the pace of testing and by April 1943 only 30 flights had been made totalling 15.25 hrs on the first prototype, while the second — first flown on 15 February 1943 at Muroc — had totalled 13.75 hrs on 24 flights and the third had still not flown. In this period, the Californian desert suffered unusually heavy rainfall, and flooding of the Rogers Dry Lake bed held up flight testing. To overcome this delay, the second XP-59A — fitted with dummy propeller and canvas covers to help preserve security — was towed 35 mls (56 km) along a public highway to Hawes Field (a satellite of what later became the George AFB) where it made one flight on 11 March. Because of worries about security, however, the aircraft was then moved to Harpers Lake, some few miles distant, where it remained until 7 April. Once this aircraft had returned to Muroc, the rate of flight testing began to accelerate, helped also by the third prototype which joined the programme late in April.

Bell, meanwhile, was into production of a service test batch of 13 YP-59As that had been ordered on 26 March 1943. These aircraft were substantially the same as the prototypes in external appearance but had rearward-sliding, instead of sideways-hinged, cockpit canopies; they were intended to be powered by the improved General Electric I-16 (later J31) turbojet with a rating of 1,650 lb st (748 kgp) compared with the 1,300 lb st (590 kgp) or so actually produced by the I-A engines. The USAAF also directed that the final four YP-59As should each have an armament of one 37-mm cannon and three 0.50-in (12,7-mm) machine guns, all in the nose, instead of the two-cannon armament that would be retained by the first nine YP-59As.

The first two YP-59As reached Muroc in June 1943 and the first flight was made there (by the second aircraft) on 18 August 1943, I-A engines being fitted because the I-16s were not yet ready. With these lower rated engines, the aircraft demonstrated a speed of 389 mph (626 km/h) at 35,160 ft (10 717 m) and 350 mph (563 km/h) at sea level, the gross weight being 8,900 lb (4 037 kg). Time to reach 30,000 ft (9 145 m) was 18.82 mins. Installation of I-16s in the YP-59A in due course increased the maximum speed to 409 mph (658 km/h) at 35,000 ft (10 675 m).

The first YP-59A was the second to fly, this event taking place at Muroc on 15 September 1943, and in due course aircraft nos 4, 5, 6 and 7 also were delivered to the Muroc test base for final assembly and flight test. The third YP-59A, meanwhile, had been shipped to Britain to permit evaluation of the Bell design alongside the Gloster Meteor (an example of which was sent to the USA in exchange). It was assembled by Gloster at Moreton Valance, where Bell test pilot Frank H Kelley Jr made the first flight in it on 28 September 1943. In full RAF camouflage and with the serial number RJ362/G, this YP-59A was transferred to the RAE Farnborough by Wg Cdr H J Wilson (who had earlier visited Muroc to become the first Briton to fly the Bell jet fighter, in April 1943) on 5 November, but only 11 flights were made on it up to April 1944 and it was returned to the USA early in 1945, plans for a

17

production model P-59B to be tested in England then being dropped.

Of the remaining YP-59As of the service test and evaluation batch, Nos 8 and 9 were assigned to the US Navy in November 1942, No 10 was converted to a drone to help in the development of radio control equipment for other aircraft and was lost on 23 March 1945 in a radio-controlled take-off, Nos 11 and 12 were assigned to NACA for full-scale wind tunnel tests, respectively at Langley Field and Cleveland and the last, No 13, after being used for gunnery tests in April 1944, was converted to a drone controller, with a second cockpit in the nose as first developed for the XP-59A. The second-cockpit modification was also applied to the seventh YP-59A and the third XP-59A in the course of their testing at Muroc.

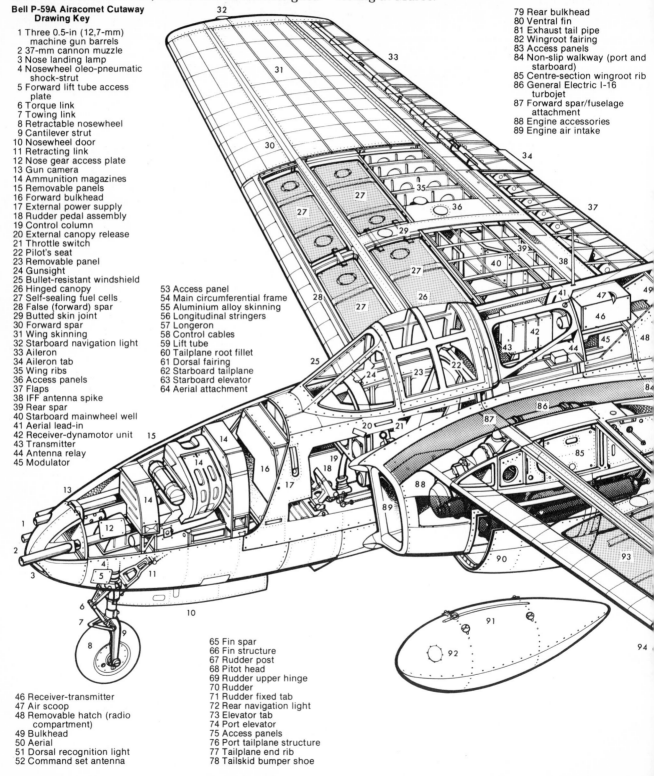

Bell P-59A Airacomet Cutaway Drawing Key

1 Three 0.5-in (12,7-mm) machine gun barrels
2 37-mm cannon muzzle
3 Nose landing lamp
4 Nosewheel oleo-pneumatic shock-strut
5 Forward lift tube access plate
6 Torque link
7 Towing link
8 Retractable nosewheel
9 Cantilever strut
10 Nosewheel door
11 Retracting link
12 Nose gear access plate
13 Gun camera
14 Ammunition magazines
15 Removable panels
16 Forward bulkhead
17 External power supply
18 Rudder pedal assembly
19 Control column
20 External canopy release
21 Throttle switch
22 Pilot's seat
23 Removable panel
24 Gunsight
25 Bullet-resistant windshield
26 Hinged canopy
27 Self-sealing fuel cells
28 False (forward) spar
29 Butted skin joint
30 Forward spar
31 Wing skinning
32 Starboard navigation light
33 Aileron
34 Aileron tab
35 Wing ribs
36 Access panels
37 Flaps
38 IFF antenna spike
39 Rear spar
40 Starboard mainwheel well
41 Aerial lead-in
42 Receiver-dynamotor unit
43 Transmitter
44 Antenna relay
45 Modulator

46 Receiver-transmitter
47 Air scoop
48 Removable hatch (radio compartment)
49 Bulkhead
50 Aerial
51 Dorsal recognition light
52 Command set antenna

53 Access panel
54 Main circumferential frame
55 Aluminium alloy skinning
56 Longitudinal stringers
57 Longeron
58 Control cables
59 Lift tube
60 Tailplane root fillet
61 Dorsal fairing
62 Starboard tailplane
63 Starboard elevator
64 Aerial attachment

65 Fin spar
66 Fin structure
67 Rudder post
68 Pitot head
69 Rudder upper hinge
70 Rudder
71 Rudder fixed tab
72 Rear navigation light
73 Elevator tab
74 Port elevator
75 Access panels
76 Port tailplane structure
77 Tailplane end rib
78 Tailskid bumper shoe

79 Rear bulkhead
80 Ventral fin
81 Exhaust tail pipe
82 Wingroot fairing
83 Access panels
84 Non-slip walkway (port and starboard)
85 Centre-section wingroot rib
86 General Electric I-16 turbojet
87 Forward spar/fuselage attachment
88 Engine accessories
89 Engine air intake

The gunnery trials with YP-59A No 13 covered the firing only of the three machine guns, in dives at speeds from 220 mph (354 km/h) to 340 mph (547 km/h) and they showed that poor directional stability at speeds above 290 mph (467 km/h) made the Airacomet — as the Bell fighter was named in September 1943 — a poor gun platform. Spinning trials were started late in December 1943 and led to the introduction of a small

90 Engine access removable panels
91 Auxiliary drop tank
92 Fuel filler cap
93 Self-sealing fuel cells
94 Port mainwheel
95 Wheel fork
96 Retracting link
97 Mainwheel oleo-pneumatic shock-strut
98 Underwing shackle-type bomb (stores) rack
99 Reinforced rib
100 Mainwheel pivot
101 Filler

102 Worm and gear assembly
103 Steel forging wing spar attachment
104 Flaps
105 Aileron tab
106 Lateral stringers
107 Forward spar
108 Wing ribs
109 Rear spar
110 End rib
111 Port navigation light
112 Port aileron

ventral fin to enhance the aircraft's spin recovery characteristics, this programme being completed on 11 February 1944. On the 5th of the same month, a two-week programme of accelerated service tests began at Muroc to assess the tactical suitability of the Airacomet, three YP-59As being flown in mock combat with a P-47D Thunderbolt and P-38J Lightning. The Airacomet was found to be outclassed in performance and manoeuvrability by the piston-engined types and the report of the Army Air Forces Board on these tests concluded that the P-59 was not "operationally or tactically suited for combat" but would be "an excellent aircraft for . . . research on jet power plants and pressure cabins" and "an excellent training ship in that its low wing-loading makes the airplane very safe . . . and . . . it has two engines". Flight testing of the Airacomets came to an end at Muroc on 27 February 1944, by which time the three XP-59As and six YP-59As there had totalled 242.5 hrs with no major mishap. In June 1944, however, in the course of dive tests conducted by Bell test pilot Jack Woolams from the company's airfield at Niagara Falls, in the 10th YP-59A, the undercarriage extended suddenly and violently, breaking the downlocks, and a belly landing was made. In a continuation of the diving trials in a P-59A later that year, the entire tail unit of the aircraft broke away, Woolams escaping by parachute.

Bell had entered negotiations with the USAAF in June 1943 in respect of possible full scale production of its jet fighter and a contract for 100 P-59As was eventually confirmed on 11 March 1944 — fewer than Bell had hoped but enough for a three-squadron Fighter Group and as many as General Electric could

Bell P-59A Specification

Power Plant: Two General Electric I-16 (J31-GE-3) turbojets each rated at 1,650 lb st (748 kgp) at 16,500 rpm. Fuel capacity, 290 US gal (1 097 l) in self-sealing tanks in the wings; provision for two 150-US gal (568 l) drop tanks under wings.

Performance: Max speed, 409 mph (658 km/h) at 35,000 ft (10 670 m), 376 mph (605 km/h) at 5,000 ft (1 525 m); cruising speed (60 per cent power), 298 mph (480 km/h) at 20,000 ft (6 095 m); cruising range, 240 mls (386 km) at 20,000 ft (6 100 m); range with drop tanks, 520 mls (837 km); rate of climb, 3,200 ft/min (16,3 m/sec) at 5,000 ft (1 525 m); time to 10,000 ft (3 050 m), 3.2 min; time to 20,000 ft (6 100 m), 7.4 min; time to 30,000 ft (9 150 m), 15.5 min; service ceiling, 46,200 ft (14 090 m).

Weights: Empty, 7,950 lb (3 606 kg); normal loaded, 10,882 lb (4 909 kg); max overload, 13,000 lb (5 902 kg).

Dimensions: Span, 45 ft 6 in (13,87 m); length, 38 ft 1½ in (11,62 m); height, 12 ft 0 in (3,65 m); wing area, 386 sq ft (35,86 m²); dihedral, 3 deg 30 min; undercarriage track, 18 ft 6 in (5,64 m).

Armament: One 37-mm M4 cannon with 44 rounds and three 0.50-in (12,7-mm) machine guns with 200 rpg.

A side view (top) of the XP-59A and three-view of the P-59A.

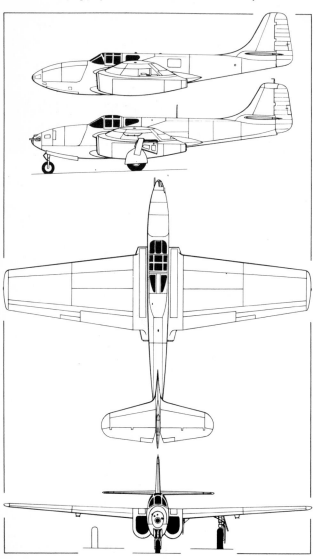

expect to provide engines for at the then rather slow rate of production. In the course of YP-59A testing, a number of modifications had been evolved, all of which were to feature on the P-59A production model. These included squared-off wing tips that reduced the span from 49 ft (14,9 m) to 45.5 ft (13,9 m) and the area from 400 sq ft (37,16 m²) to 386 sq ft (35,86 m²); a squared-off fin and rudder plus the ventral fin already mentioned; strengthened aft fuselage; metal (in place of fabric) covered flaps and ailerons, the latter being pressure balanced; up-locks for the main undercarriage legs and repositioned pitot-static tube, from under the port wing to the fin. The engines were to be I-16s, similar to those flying in the YP-59As.

Delivery of the P-59As began towards the end of 1944, but by this time the USAAF had digested the report of the evaluation earlier in the year and had decided, on 10 October, to terminate production at 39 aircraft. Because it proved more expensive to cancel than complete some airframes then nearing completion, this figure was amended to 50, of which 20 were P-59As and the final 30 were P-59Bs, distinguished by having an additional 66-US gal (250-l) bag tank in each outer wing. Delivery of the entire quantity was completed on 27 August 1945, although not all the P-59Bs originally had engines, some being stored by Bell until later in the year. Some P-59Bs were eventually fitted with 2,000 lb st (908 kg) J31-GE-5 engines.

Of the 20 P-59As, one was assigned to Wright Field, two to the AAF Proving Ground Command at Eglin Field, Florida, two to the Air Forces Board at Orlando, Florida, and one to the Extreme Temperature Operations Unit of the Cold Weather Test Unit at Ladd Field, Alaska, where it flew 69 hrs 40 min with no major problems. The remainder of the batch went to the 412th Fighter Group of the Fourth Air Force, which had formed at Muroc on 30 November 1943 to work up as the USAAF's first jet unit and had moved to Bakersfield, California, to receive the production Airacobras. Of the P-59Bs, three were assigned to the US Navy (which did not apply a separate designation to the type), one went to NACA and 19 eventually went to the 412th FG, the others remaining in storage or being used by Bell for miscellaneous tasks.

In July 1945, the 412th FG, including the 29th, 31st, 445th and 361st Fighter Squadrons, moved with its P-59As and P-59Bs to Santa Maria Army Air Field, California, where it also operated for a time the last of the YP-59As which — as already noted — had been converted to a two-seater as a drone controller and was used at Santa Maria to give flights to ground personnel. Transfering again, to March AFB, in December 1945, the 412th soon began to re-equip with the Lockheed P-80 Shooting Star; thus, the P-59 Airacomet saw little more than a year of active service and no combat deployment. To a large degree, the Bell aircraft was unsuccessful in its planned rôle as a fighter, but it served its purpose well in proving the suitability of the gas turbine as an aircraft prime mover and providing a good trainer for pilots who would soon be graduating to jet fighters of much higher performance.

(Above and below right) The sixth production Bell P-63A Kingcobra. Deliveries of this improved derivative of the Airacobra began late in 1943 and continued for a year, when the P-63C succeeded this initial version.

BELL P-63 KINGCOBRA

Despite the intensive design activity of the US aircraft manufacturers in the period immediately preceding and following America's entry into the war, and the consequent appearance of a number of prototypes, few new designs in this period achieved production status. The rapid expansion of the Army Air Corps in 1940/41 required priority to be given to the production of already-proven aircraft types and this priority was reinforced when America was brought into the armed conflict. Consequently, of nine new single-seat fighter designs flown as prototypes in 1942/43, only one was built in quantity, and even this, the Bell P-63 Kingcobra, was little more than an extrapolation of the same company's pre-war P-39 Airacobra design, and was destined almost exclusively for Lend-Lease supply to the Soviet Union.

Initial steps leading to the appearance of the P-63 had been taken by Bell in February 1941 when the company proposed combining a laminar-flow wing and uprated engine with the fuselage of a standard Airacobra. Three prototypes were ordered by the Army Air Corps in April 1941 under the designation XP-39E; at one time planned to make use of the Continental IV-1430-1 engine, they appeared in 1942 with 1,325 hp Allison V-1710-47 engines, straight-tapered wings with square tips and angular fins-and-rudders, the size and configuration of the latter differing between all three prototypes. Wing root intakes for the buried radiators were larger than for the standard P-39 and provision was retained for a cannon firing through the spinner.

Projected performance with the laminar-flow wing was promising and on 27 June 1941 — before the XP-39Es had flown — the Army ordered two prototypes of a larger development of the P-39, primarily for use as a low-level fighter-bomber and close-support aircraft,

using the same wing section and power plant (ie, the V-1710-47) but with slightly larger overall dimensions. These prototypes were designated XP-63; the first flew at Bell's plant in Buffalo, New York, on 7 December 1942 but was damaged in January 1943, shortly before the second XP-63 flew for the first time, on 5 February. This aircraft, in turn, was lost in May, by which time a third prototype, the XP-63A (ordered in June 1942) was nearing completion and the flight test programme was resumed, using this aircraft, on 26 April 1943. The

21

(Above) The P-63E Kingcobra was a 1945 model featuring an uprated engine and increased wing span but retaining the original "automobile-door" cockpit access. (Below) The single P-63D introduced a rearward sliding bubble canopy.

(Above) One of two P-63Fs, experimental models with taller fins and rudders. Note that the P-63D, E and F illustrated on this page have consecutive serial numbers. (Below) The RP-63G was produced as a unique live target, with a toughened skin and other modifications.

XP-63A differed from the first two aircraft in having a 1,325 hp V-1710-93 engine; all three prototypes could be readily distinguished from the P-39 series by their tall, straight-edged fins-and-rudders and four-bladed propellers, although the original square-cut wing tips of the XP-39Es gave way to rounded tips on the P-63 and the extra 4 ft 4 in (1,32 m) of span was not readily discernible.

The basic P-63 was designed to have an armament of one 37-mm cannon in the nose and two 0.50-in (12,7-mm) machine guns in the upper front fuselage, with provision for a 500-lb (227-kg) bomb or 75-US gal (284 l) drop tank under the fuselage; a total of 88 lb (40 kg) of armour protection was carried. Successive changes and improvements in the armament, armour and fuel load were made in production P-63As, built under a contract placed on 29 September 1942 and delivered from October 1943 onwards. Among these changes, distinguished by block numbers from P-63A-1 to P-63A-10, were provision for a flush-fitting ferry fuel tank of 175 US gal (662 l) capacity; provision of wing bomb racks to take up to 522-lb (237-kg) each side, or fuel tanks; the addition of a 0.50-in (12,7-mm) machine gun pack beneath each wing, with a total of 900 rounds for the wing and fuselage guns; an increase from 30 to 58 rounds for the nose cannon; provision for six underwing rocket projectiles and progressive increases in armour weight to 179 lb (81 kg), 189 lb (86 kg), 199 lb (90 kg) and eventually 266 lb (121 kg).

Bell delivered 1,725 P-63As between October 1943 and December 1944 and then went on to produce 1,227 P-63Cs, which differed in having the 1,325 hp V-1710-117 engine with increased war emergency power rating, and a long shallow ventral fin. Internal fuel capacity was increased from 100 to 107 US gal (379 to 405 l) and the weight of armour protection was 201 lb (91,3 kg); armament remained unchanged. The XP-63B designation had covered the planned installation of a Packard-Merlin V-1650-5 engine in the XP-63A prototype, but this did not materialize.

A single P-63D was a P-63C modified early in 1945 to

have a 1,425 hp V-1710-109 engine, modified wings with 10-in (25,4-cm) span increase and a rearward-sliding bubble canopy. Thirteen P-63Es were similar, but retained the standard Kingcobra cockpit with built-up rear fairing and "automobile-door" access; production of 2,930 on order when the war ended was cancelled, but two other airframes covered by the same contract emerged as P-63Fs, with 1,425 hp V-1710-135 engines and taller fins-and-rudders. Despite increases in gross weight, to a maximum of 11,200 lb (5 085 kg) for the P-63E, these late-model Kingcobras had considerably improved performance: the P-63D, for example, achieved 437 mph (703 km/h) at 30,000 ft (9 150 m) compared with the P-63A's 408 mph (656 km/h) at 24,450 ft (7 457 m). This, however, was in 1945, by which time the operational requirement to which the aircraft had been designed was outdated.

Few USAAF units equipped on the Kingcobra, and those that did remained on advanced training status in the USA, seeing no action overseas. Of a grand total of 3,303 P-63s of all types produced by Bell, 2,421, or more than two-thirds, were assigned to the Soviet Union through Lend-Lease arrangements. Of the total, 21 were lost en route to Russia, delivery being made by air from the assembly point at Great Falls, Montana. Responsibility for this major supply effort (which handled 6,000 of a total 15,000 or so US aircraft delivered to the Soviet Union between June 1941 and September 1945) was vested in the 7th Ferrying Group, the Alaskan Division of the Air Transport Command, whose pilots collected P-63s from Bell's factory close to the Niagara Falls and flew them to Great Falls for winterization. They were then flown north across Canada to Fairbanks, Alaska, which was the jumping-off point for the flight into the Soviet Union, final destination usually being an airfield near Moscow.

Although the USAAF found no operational use for the Kingcobra, the Soviet Air Forces apparently

One of the two Kingcobras supplied to Britain and used for aerodynamic research at the RAE Farnborough.

obtained good results with the Bell fighter in its intended rôle of a close-support aircraft. Its built-in armament and external bomb-load gave it a heavy punch when ground-strafing, its overall performance at low-to-medium altitudes was good and it revealed a rugged ability to absorb battle damage and remain airborne.

The only operational deployment of the P-63 outside

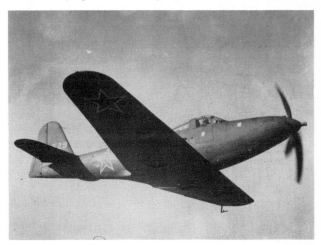

(Above right) A Kingcobra (minus guns in the underwing fairings) in the markings of the Soviet Air Force, which was the major user of the type. (Below) Bell P-63Cs with belly fuel tanks and underwing bomb racks, in service with the Armée de l'Air in 1945.

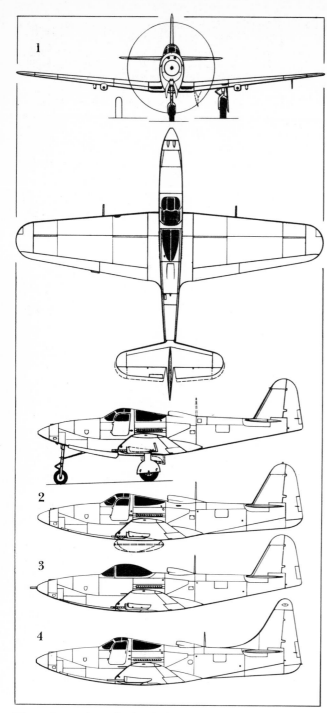

Kingcobra variants depicted above are (1), The P-63A; (2), the P-63C with ventral fin and (optional) underwing and belly racks; (3), the P-63D with revised canopy and (4), the P-63F with extended fin and rudder.

of Russia came with the supply, in mid-1945, of 300 P-63Cs to the *Armée de l'Air*. Too late for combat use in Europe, they did see some operational service in France's subsequent involvement in Indo-China. Two P-63As were supplied to Britan, through Lend-Lease, to permit evaluation of the type by the RAF, but like the USAAF, the latter found no operational use for the Kingcobra. Both British examples were used at the

RAE, Farnborough, for research programmes concerned with the behaviour of laminar-flow wings — the first (FR408) from May to August 1944 and the second (FZ440, with a clear-view one-piece canopy) from April 1945 onwards.

During 1943, with production of the P-63 in full swing but no clear operational need for the type in USAAF service, the Kingcobra became the subject of an intriguing scheme to use manned aircraft as 'live' targets. The idea was to use target aircraft with specially reinforced surface skins in conjunction with frangible bullets fired by the training aircraft which, upon hitting the targets, shattered harmlessly. With the designation RP-63A-11, five Kingcobras were stripped of all armament and internal armour, and re-skinned; a clam-shell intake replaced the usual dorsal intake to the centrally-mounted engine to reduce its vulnerability. An additional unique feature of the RP-63As, which were the first aircraft actually designed to be shot at for training purposes other than under remote control, was an automatic recording system that also flashed the aircraft's landing lights every time the target received a hit; hardly surprisingly, the RP-63As quickly became known as Pinball targets!

Successful tests with the first five aircraft led to production of a further 95 RP-63A-12s, which had increased internal tankage. Bell then built 200 RP-63Cs, which had the V-1710-117 engine, and Kingcobra production ended with 32 RP-63Gs having V-1710-135 engines, a further 420 of the latter model being cancelled. Although never flown as pilotless drones, the target Kingcobras were later re-designated in the drone category as QF-63A, QF-63C and QF-63G respectively. Of the total production of 3,303 Kingcobras, including prototypes, therefore, 2,421 were assigned to the Soviet Union, 300 to France and two to Britain, and of the 580 that remained, 332 were targets for USAAF use and the other 248 were used for various experimetal and non-combat purposes.

Bell P-63A Specification

Power Plant: One Allison V-1710-93 liquid-cooled 12-cylinder Vee engine, rated at 1,325 hp for take-off and 1,150 hp at 22,400 ft (6 832 m) with a war emergency rating of 1,500 hp at sea level. Fuel capacity, 100 US gal (379 l) internal plus provision for one 175-US gal (662-l) ferry tank or three 75-US gal (284-l) drop tanks.

Performance: Max speed, 361 mph (581 km/h) at 5,000 ft (1 525 m), 392 mph (631 km/h) at 15,000 ft (4 575 m), 410 mph (660 km/h) at 25,000 ft (7 625 m); max cruising speed, 378 mph (608 km/h); time to 25,000 ft (7 625 m), 7.3 min; service ceiling, 43,000 ft (13 115 m); range, 390-450 mls (628-724 km); ferry range, 2,575 mls (4 143 km).

Weights: Empty, 6,375 lb (2 894 kg); normal loaded, 8,800 lb (3 995 kg); max gross, 10,500 lb (4 767 kg).

Dimensions: Span, 38 ft 4 in (11,69 m); length, 32 ft 8 in (9,96 m); height, 12 ft 7 in (3,84 m); wing area, 248 sq ft (23,04 m²).

Armament: One 37-mm cannon firing through spinner, with 58 rounds; two 0.50-in (12,7-mm) machine guns in upper front fuselage and two in underwing fairings with total of 900 rounds; one bomb rack under fuselage and one under each wing for up to 522-lb (237-kg) bombs.

The second and last Bell XP-77, developed in 1942 as a radical attempt to build a lightweight fighter of "non-strategic" materials. Original promise of the design was not fulfilled.

BELL XP-77

The rapid expansion of aircraft production, together with other armaments, in the USA in the period from 1939 to 1941, inevitably led to shortages in the supply of some materials and there were fears that some of these shortages might become critical. Interest therefore began to be focussed upon the substitution of non-critical materials for those in short supply, a typical example being wood in place of light alloy for aircraft construction. Discussions between USAAF personnel and engineers of the Bell Aircraft Corp began in October 1941 at Wright Field with a view to developing a lightweight "non-strategic" fighter and led to the eventual construction of two prototypes of the XP-77.

Initially referred to as the Tri-4 and later by the Bell design designation D-6, the XP-77 was a very small low wing monoplane using resin-bonded laminated wood construction with a stressed skin. It had an electrically-operated tricycle undercarriage, electric flaps and hydraulic brakes. The engine was a 520 hp Ranger V-770 — a 12-cylinder air-cooled in-line unit that was intended to be developed in a supercharged version (the XV-770-9) for the XP-77 but in fact was only available in the unsupercharged XV-770-7 form. Bell initially planned an armament of one 20-mm cannon firing through the propeller hub and two 0.50-in (12,7-mm) machine guns in the forward fuselage and expected to achieve a gross weight of 3,700 lb (1 680 kg) and a max speed of 410 mph (660 km/h) at 27,000 ft (8 235 m) using the supercharged engine. The USAAF, however, requested provision for a 300-lb (136-kg) bomb or 325-lb (148-kg) depth charge to be carried, and the nose cannon was abandoned.

Six prototypes of the XP-77 were ordered on 29 September 1942, plus two static test airframes, a mock-up and a full-scale model for wind-tunnel testing. Bell's other commitments, however — which included production of the P-39 and P-63 and, eventually, development of the P-59 jet fighter — limited the effort that could be expended on the XP-77, and this, combined with the lack of a supercharged engine, growth in the bare weight of the prototypes, reduced performance estimates, overrunning costs and increasing supplies of light alloys led to interest in the XP-77 programme waning during 1943. The contract was reduced to only two flying prototypes in August 1943 and the first of these was not ready for flight test until 1 April 1944, delays having occurred in the manufacture of the wings and fuselage, which had been

(Above) The second and (below) the first XP-77. The former was lost during flight testing in 1944.

(Above) The very small dimensions of the Bell XP-77 are emphasised by this view of the first prototype, scale being given by the cockpit. (Below left) A three-view drawing of the XP-77.

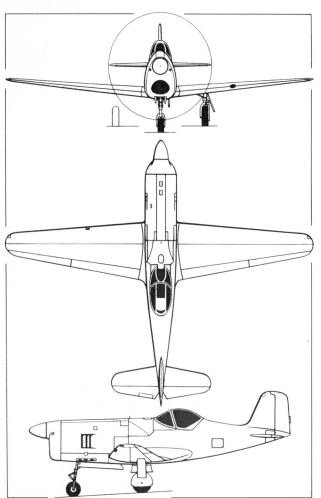

subcontracted by Bell to Vidal Research Corporation.

Both prototypes of the XP-77 were tested briefly by the USAAF in 1944, the second aircraft being lost on 2 October 1944 when it entered an inverted spin and the pilot bailed out. The entire development contract was terminated in December 1944, the consensus of opinion being that the XP-77 was operationally unsuitable and that its performance showed no improvements over heavier fighters of conventional construction.

Bell XP-77 Specification

Power Plant: One 520 hp Ranger XV-770-7 twelve-cylinder inverted-Vee air cooled engine driving an Aeroproducts two-bladed propeller of 9 ft 6 in (29-m) diameter. Fuel capacity, 52 US gal (197 l) in fuselage tank between engine firewall and cockpit. Provision for one 38-US gal (144-l) auxiliary tank on fuselage centreline.

Performance: Max speed, 330 mph (531 km/h) at 4,000 ft (1 220 m), 328 mph (528 km/h) at 12,600 ft (3 843 m); typical operating speed, 274 mph (441 km/h); initial rate of climb, 3,600 ft/min (18,3 m/sec); time to 9,000 ft (2 745 m), 3.7 min; service ceiling, 30,100 ft (9 180 m); range, 305 mls (491 km) on internal fuel at max speed, 550 mls (885 km) at 274 mph (386 km/h).

Weights: Empty, 2,855 lb (1 296 kg); design gross, 3,672 lb (1 667 kg); max gross (with 325-lb/148-kg store), 4,028 lb (1 829 kg).

Dimensions: Span, 27 ft 6 in (8,39 m); length, 22 ft 10½ in (6,98 m); height, 8 ft 2¼ in (2,49 m); wing area, 100 sq ft (9,29 m²); dihedral, 5 deg constant.

Armament: Two 0.50-in (12,7-mm) M-2 Colt-Browning machine guns in upper forward fuselage with 200 rpg. Fuselage centreline pylon with provision for one 100-lb or 300-lb (45-kg or 136-kg) bomb or one 250-lb (113-kg) or 325-lb (148-kg) depth charge.

BELL XP-83

Based on experience gained with the P-59 Airacomet, Bell Aircraft Corp began, early in 1944, the development of a fighter of similar configuration but improved overall performance. In particular, attention was given to increasing the range, which was a critical aspect of the performance of most early jet fighters. The new Bell fighter was made the subject of a USAAF development contract awarded on 31 July 1944, covering the construction of two prototypes to be designated XP-83.

The XP-83 retained the same layout as used in the P-59, with two engines tucked into fuselage-side locations beneath the mid-mounted wing — a layout that minimized the asymmetric effects of a possible engine failure, and left the maximum space available in the fuselage for fuel and armament. The XP-83 in fact had an internal fuel capacity of 1,095 US gal (4 145 l), which could be supplemented by two 300-US gal (1 135-l) drop tanks. Armament was grouped in the short nose ahead of the pressurized cockpit and in the prototypes comprised six 0.50-in (12,7-mm) machine guns, although there were also schemes for mounting a battery of 20 such weapons, or four 20-mm or 37-mm cannon.

The first XP-83 flew on 25 February 1945, but the performance proved somewhat disappointing and with more promising fighters already under development, the Bell XP-83 — which proved to be the company's final war-time fighter design — was abandoned. Construction was of metal throughout, the wing being a two-spar structure, and the fuselage a semi-monocoque; covering was by stressed skin. Fowler flaps were fitted and the ailerons were power assisted.

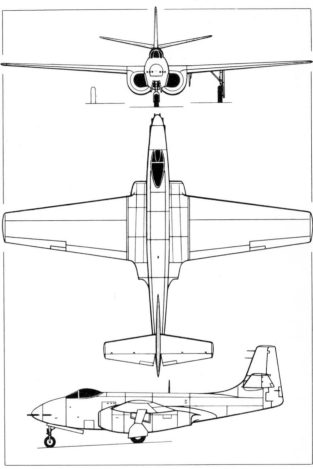

Bell XP-83 Specification

Power Plant: Two General Electric J33-GE-5 turbojets each rated at 4,000 lb st (1 816 kgp) for take-off at 11,500 rpm.
Performance: Max speed, 522 mph (840 km/h) at 15,660 ft (4 776 m); initial rate of climb, 5,650 ft/min (28,7 m/sec); time to 30,000 ft (9 150 m), 11½ min; range, 1,730 mls (2 784 km) on internal fuel, 2,050 mls (3 298 km) with two drop tanks.
Weights: Empty, 14,105 lb (6 404 kg); normal gross, 24,090 lb (10 937 kg); max overload, 27,500 lb (12 485 kg).
Dimensions: Span, 53 ft 0 in (16,17 m); length, 44 ft 10 in (13,68 m); height, 15 ft 3 in (4,65 m); wing area, 431 sq ft (40,04 m²).
Armament: Six 0.50-in (12,7-mm) machine guns in nose with 300 rpg. Provision for one 1,000-lb (454-kg) bomb under each wing.

(Below) the prototype Bell XP-83 long-range jet fighter, tested early in 1945 but soon abandoned. (Above right) A three-view drawing of the XP-83.

CONVAIR XP-81

Like the US Navy (with the Curtiss XF15C-1 and the Ryan FR-1), the USAAF investigated the practicability of combining the advantages of the pure jet engine for high performance with a piston engine or a turboprop to obtain increased range. With a view to producing an escort fighter suitable, in particular, for operations in the Pacific area, two prototypes were ordered from Consolidated Vultee Aircraft Corporation on 11 February 1944 of a long-range fighter with a General Electric TG-100 turboprop in the nose and an Allison J33-GE-5 turbojet in the rear fuselage. The former would be used for endurance cruissing and the latter to boost performance in the target area.

Convair's first jet fighter design, the XP-81, as the type was designated, featured a low wing, tricycle

The XP-81 prototype after it had been fitted with the definitive TG-100 turboprop in the nose.

The upper side view in the drawing below depicts the Convair XP-81 as first flown with piston engine and the other three views show the projected production version.

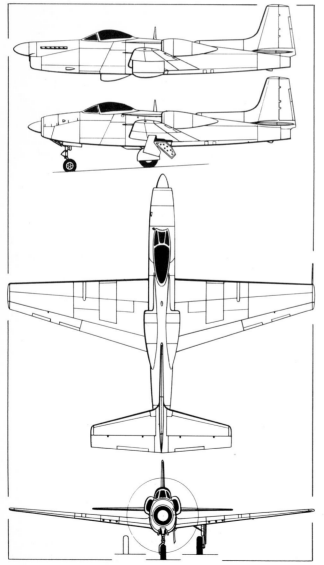

undercarriage and a pair of dorsal intakes behind the cockpit to supply air to the turbojet in the rear fuselage. The turboprop in the nose had a short tailpipe, exhausting behind the nosewheel and beneath the cockpit. Completed in January 1945, the first XP-81 was delayed by non-availability of the TG-100 turboprop (later designated XT31-GE-1) and to allow flight testing to begin, a Packard V-1650-7 Merlin from a P-51D was installed at short notice, the radiator occupying the space allowed for the tailpipe of the TG-100. In this form, the XP-81 was transferred to Muroc where it was flown for the first time on 11 February 1945, showing excellent handling characteristics.

The progress of the war in the Pacific and projected refinement of turbojets that promised lower fuel consumption and, therefore, greater range, led to a waning of interest in the Convair project, however, and although Convair had completed 85 per cent of the engineering for a batch of 13 service-test YP-81s, this contract was cancelled shortly before VJ-Day. The YP-81 was intended to have the more powerful TG-110 turboprop and some airframe changes. The sole XP-81 completed was eventually fitted with the TG-100 and first flew in this guise on 21 December 1945. The data below are estimated for the developed version of the design.

Convair XP-81 Specification
Power Plant: One 2,300 ehp General Electric XT31-GE-1 turboprop and one 3,750 lb st (1 703 kgp) Allison J33-GE-5 turbojet. Fuel capacity, 811 US gal (3 070 l) plus provision for two 350-US gal (1 325-l) drop tanks.
Performance: Max speed, 478 mph (769 km/h) at sea level, 507 mph (816 km/h) at 30,000 ft (9 150 m); cruising speed, 275 mph (442 km/h) at 25,000 ft (7 625 m); initial rate of climb, 5,300 ft/min (26,9 m/sec); service ceiling, 35,500 ft (10 828 m); range, 2,500 mls (4 023 km).
Weights: Empty, 12,755 lb (5 790 kg); normal loaded, 19,500 lb (8 853 kg); max overload, 24,650 lb (11 190 kg).
Dimensions: Span, 50 ft 6 in (15,4 m); length, 44 ft 10 in (13,69 m); height, 14 ft 0 in (4,27 m); wing area, 425 sq ft (39,5 m²).
Armament: Six 0.50-in (12,7-mm) machine guns in the wings with 300 rpg plus alternative provision for six 20-mm cannon; up to 3,200 lb (1 453 kg) of bombs under wings.

CURTISS HAWK 75
(P-36 AND MOHAWK)

Among the aircraft equipping pursuit squadrons of the US Army Air Force based in Hawaii in December 1941, at the time of the Japanese attack, were a number of Curtiss P-36s (together with Bell P-39s and Curtiss P-40s, also described in this volume). Primarily, the P-36s were serving with the 46th and 47th Pursuit Squadrons of the 15th Pursuit Group at Wheeler Field, the 45th Squadron having already converted to P-40s at the same base, and although many of the Group's aircraft were destroyed on the ground in the first attack, a few P-36s of the two squadrons took off and succeeded in intercepting a formation of nine Japanese aircraft, of which two were destroyed. Thus, the P-36 gained the distinction of achieving the Army Air Force's first victories in air-to-air combat in World War II. By co-incidence, a variant of this same Curtiss fighter, more than two years previously, had also gained the first Allied aerial victories over Europe when two Messerschmitt Bf 109s were shot down by Hawk 75s of the French *Groupe de Chasse* II/4.

The monoplane responsible for these two historic fighting successes was far from being the best available either in Europe or in the Pacific area by the time these engagements took place, but at the time its design had been started in 1934 it represented a determined effort by Curtiss to retain its position in the forefront of fighter aircraft manufacturers. This reputation had been won with a series of biplanes sharing the generic appellation of Hawk, which for many years had constituted the equipment of many front-line squadrons of both the US Army Air Corps and the US Navy, as well as providing Curtiss with useful export business.

The catalyst for the design of the first Curtiss monoplane fighter to enter production was an Army Air Corps specification issued in 1934 and calling for an all-metal low-wing design with a top speed of 300 mph (482 km/h). This specification was to bring responses, in the next two years, from five companies (Seversky, Northrop, Consolidated and Vought as well as Curtiss) and would lead to production of two new fighters for the Army. For the Curtiss Aeroplane and Motor Company (a division of Curtiss-Wright Corporation, renamed simply the Curtiss Aeroplane Division of C-W on 1 January 1936) the specification represented a special challenge, for its position had already been eroded by Boeing with the P-26, the first "modern" monoplane fighter sold to the Air Corps, and the Curtiss management was aware that its engineering department needed an infusion of design talent in order to breeak free of its set ideas on biplane fighter design. Such talent was found in Donovan R Berlin, who had gained experience of stressed skin design working onthe Northrop Alpha, Beta and Gamma series of monoplanes but had left Northrop earlier in 1934. During October, Don Berlin joined Curtiss at Buffalo, NY, having only seven months in which to design and build a prototype of the new fighter within the Army's

(Above) The Curtiss Model 75 as first flown with the two-row Wright XR-1670 radial engine and (below) re-engined with the single-row Pratt & Whitney R-1535.

deadline for trials to be conducted at Wright Field, on 27 May 1935.

Berlin's design — identified by Curtiss as Design 75, although model numbers had not previously been used by the company — was for a relatively small monoplane of clean and simple lines, avoiding complex manufacturing techniques and emphasising ease of maintenance. With no revolutionary features, the Curtiss 75 conformed to the contemporary ideas of fighter designers in several other countries, many of whom were working on aircraft of generally similar configuration. Berlin's design team adopted an aluminium alloy monocoque fuselage — built in two halves and mated after installation of internal components — and a multi-spar metal wing with flush-riveted smooth Alclad skinning. The aerofoil section was chosen from the newly developed NACA 2200 series, with a t/c ratio of 15 per cent at the root. The aircraft had hydraulically-actuated split flaps and undercarriage, the mainwheels pivoting (in accordance with a patented Boeing design) about their axes to lie flush in the wing, and an aft-sliding cockpit canopy. Armament, as required by the specification, comprised two machine guns, one 0.30-in (7,62-mm) and one 0.50-in (12,7-mm), in the upper front fuselage, firing through the airscrew disc.

The key to success for the new fighter was clearly going to depend upon use of a satisfactory engine, and Curtiss chose to use a new two-row 14-cylinder radial that Wright had under development as the XR-1670, with a promised 900 hp output and small frontal area. Bearing the civil registration (N)X17Y, the Curtiss Model 75 made its first flight in mid-April 1935, but the engine proved unsatisfactory and, as none of the other prototypes intended for the Army competition was ready for testing, the Air Corps postponed the deadline from May to August 1935. This gave Curtiss time to

One of the three Y1P-36s built by Curtiss for USAAC evaluation in 1937, these being substantially the same as the Model 75B prototype apart from using the R-1830 Twin Wasp engine.

substitute a Pratt & Whitney R-1535 Twin Wasp Junior, but this engine also gave considerable trouble; with the other contestants also suffering their share of difficulties, the Air Corps again postponed the contest, to April 1936, and the Model 75 was given its third engine installation in 12 months with the fitting of a 950 hp Wright XR-1820-39 Cyclone single-row nine-cylinder unit, becoming known as the Model 75B in this guise. Neither the Model 75B nor its principal competitor, the Seversky SEV-1XP, achieved the magic 300 mph (482 km/h) performance, and both continued to be dogged by engine problems, being unable to obtain full power. However, the Army believed the Seversky monoplane showed enough promise to award it a contract for 77 production models as the P-35A; the Curtiss 75B was rated second and given a "consolation prize" in the form of a contract for three service test versions designated Y1P-36. These, the Army specified, were to be powered by the Pratt & Whitney R-1830 Twin Wasp, a 14-cylinder two-row radial that showed every sign of being able to produce the 900 hp that Berlin had originally expected from the R-1670.

The first Y1P-36 was completed in February 1937, being substantially the same as the Model 75B apart from the R-1830-13 engine with a take-off rating of 1,050 hp and giving 900 hp at 12,000 ft (3 660 m); the cockpit was modified with a raised top line and improved rear view by increasing the "scalloping" in the rear decking, the tail wheel was made retractable and armament was fitted for the first time. Gross weight of the Y1P-36 came out at 5,437 lb (2 468 kg) compared with the Model 75B's 5,075 lb (2 304 kg) and a speed of 294.5 mph (474 km/h) was recorded in trials at Wright Field in May 1937, some 10 mph (16 km/h) better than the prototype. The Y1P-36 also demonstrated excellent flying characteristics, with good manoeuvrability, and received enthusiastic comments from Army test pilots; these characteristics were to endear the Curtiss fighter to

many pilots who would take it into combat in the next few years.

On the basis of this evaluation, the Army Air Corps decided to order the Curtiss fighter into production, placing a contract on 7 July 1937 for 210 aircraft at a cost of $4,113,550 — the largest single contract the Army Air Corps had placed since the end of World War I. Deliveries began in April 1938, with 177 of the total order being completed to P-36A standard. These aircraft differed from the Y1P-36 in having a Curtiss Electric constant speed propeller instead of the Hamilton Standard unit. Armament was unchanged, with 200 rounds for the 0.50-in (12,7-mm) Browning and 500 rounds for the smaller weapon and the normal fuel capacity of 87 Imp gal (395 l) could be increased to an overload condition with 135 Imp gal (613 l). The gross weight of the P-36A was 5,470 lb (2 481 kg), or 6,010 lb (2 726 kg) in overload condition, and the maximum speed was 300 mph (483 km/h) at 10,000 ft (6 100 m).

Many teething problems were encountered as the Air Corps attempted to work up its first squadrons on the P-36A, these being the 55th, 77th and 79th Pursuit Squadrons of the 20th Pursuit Group at Barksdale Field. Severe skin buckling occurred in the wings in the area of the wheel wells, leading to the introduction of thicker skins and reinforcing webs, and the fuselage structure also showed some signs of weakness, while the engine exhaust system proved to be a constant source of trouble. The P-36A was grounded more than once during 1938, and at one time the 20th PG, which had previously flown Boeing P-26s, was down to six serviceable aircraft, all of which were restricted to 250 mph (402 km/h) with a ban on manoeuvres. As the slow and laborious process to overcome these problems proceeded into 1939, additional units began converting onto the type — the 4th and 27th Pursuit Squadrons of the 1st Pursuit Group at Selfridge Field, Mich, and the

33rd, 35th and 36th Pursuit Squadrons of the 8th PG at Mitchell Field, NY.

Only the first 14 P-36As had the R-1830-13 engine, a switch then being made to the R-1830-17 with a higher compression ratio, rated at 1,200 hp for take-off and 1,050 hp at 6,500 ft (1 983 m). This same engine was used in the 30 P-36Cs that completed the production batch of Curtiss Model 75s for the Army Air Corps, the distinguishing feature of this version being the addition of a 0.30-in (7,62-mm) machine gun in each wing, indicated externally by the cartridge case collecting boxes that protruded beneath the wings just outboard of the wheel stowage. Maximum speed of the P-36A with the -17 engine increased to 313 mph (504 km/h) at 10,000 ft (3 050 m); the P-36C, with a gross weight of 6,150 lb (2 792 kg) and the external cartridge case collectors, was 2 mph (3,2 km/h) slower. Both versions had a range of about 820 mls (1 320 km) cruising at about 270 mph (434 km/h).

Included in the production quantity of 210 aircraft were three airframes completed to different standards. The fourth production airframe became the single example of the XP-42 when it was fitted with an R-1830-31 engine with a extended engine mounting, casing and propeller shaft, producing a streamlined, fully-enclosed engine installation. First flown in March 1939, the XP-42 achieved 315 mph (552 km/h) but suffered severe cooling problems; the latter were partially alleviated when a NACA-developed D-type cowl was fitted, reducing the length by 13 in (33 cm), and a speed of 343 mph (552 km/h) was achieved in May 1941 but the XP-42 remained entirely experimental.

The 10th P-36 airframe was completed as the prototype XP-40 (see page 48) and the 20th emerged as the P-36B when fitted with a 1,100 hp R-1830-25 engine, this aircraft later reverting to P-36A standard. Other P-36As were withdrawn from service after delivery for experimental purposes, mostly concerned with armament experiments. These included the XP-36D in September 1939, with 0.50-in (12,7-mm) guns in both front fuselage bays and 0.30-in (7,62-mm) guns in the wings; the XP-36E with four 0.30-in (7,62-mm) guns in the wings and the XP-36F with the standard nose armament plus a 23-mm Madsen cannon in a fairing under each wing. The wing guns adopted for the P-36C were also first tested in a P-36A which thus became in effect the prototype P-36C. One P-36A was tested at Wright Field with a fixed landing gear incorporating streamlined skis designed by Luscombe; this was for possible use in Alaskan operations but when P-36s were eventually assigned to that area, they retained the normal landing gear.

After its use for evaluation at Wright Field, the original Y1P-36 also became a test bed, flying with a four-bladed propeller and then with two-bladed contra-props — the first such installation on a US aircraft. Another prototype tested by the Army in 1938 was the company-owned Model 75R, built as a demonstrator with a Pratt & Whitney R-1830-19 engine fitted with a turbo-supercharger beneath the nose, just aft of the engine cowling, with a ventrally-mounted inter-cooler. This installation proved unreliable in operation, however and, lacking automatic controls, imposed a heavy work load on the pilot during combat. This

(Above right) A P-36A in the overall drab and grey finish adopted by the USAAC in 1941, serving with the 16th Squadron, 51st Pursuit Group as a trainer. (Below) A P-36A serving with the 79th Squadron of the 20th Pursuit Group — the first unit to receive the P-36.

Curtiss P-36A Specification

Power Plant: One Pratt & Whitney R-1830-17 Twin Wasp 14-cylinder two-row air-cooled radial engine rated at 1,200 hp at 2,700 rpm for take-off and 1,050 hp at 2,550 hp at 6,500 ft (1 983 m). Curtiss Electric three-blade constant speed fully-feathering propeller, diameter 10 ft (3,05 m); fuel capacity, 162 US gal (613 l) in two tanks in wings and auxiliary tank in fuselage.

Performance: Max speed, 313 mph (504 km/h) at 10,000 ft (3 050 m); initial rate of climb, 2,600 ft/min (13,2 m/sec); time to 15,000 ft (4 575 m), 4.8 min; service ceiling, 33,700 ft (10 280 m); normal range, 825 mls (1 327 km).

Weights: Empty, 4,567 lb (2 073 kg); normal loaded, 5,650 lb (2 565 kg); max gross, 6,010 lb (2 728 kg).

Dimensions: Span, 37 ft 4 in (11,39 m); length, 28 ft 6 in (8,70 m); height, 12 ft 2 in (3,70 m); wing area, 236 sq ft (21,92 m²); under-carriage track, 8 ft 1 in (2,47 m).

Armament: One 0.30-in (7,62-mm) machine gun with 500 rounds and one 0.50-in (12,7-mm) machine gun with 200 rounds in upper front fuselage decking.

prototype (with the civil registration NX 22028) participated in the Air Corps fighter competition at Wright Field in January 1939, which was won by the Curtiss P-40, and demonstrated a top speed of 330 mph (531 km/h) at 15,000 ft (4 570 m) but the turbo-supercharger was later removed and the aircraft was used for other purposes by the company, at one time being fitted with a Cyclone engine.

As already noted, P-36As had entered service, somewhat tentatively, with squadrons of the 1st, 8th and 20th Pursuit Groups during 1938 and 1939. As additional aircraft became available and the teething problems were overcome, the Curtiss fighter began to see wider service within the Air Corps which, as of the end of 1940, had six Pursuit Groups. In addition to the 1st, 8th and 20th these comprised the 15th, 16th and 18th Pursuit Group, and P-36s flew with at least some of the squadrons of each of these three Groups in the period 1940/41. Of these Groups, the 16th was assigned to the Panama Canal Zone and the 15th and 18th were stationed in Hawaii, where the P-36s began to arrive early in 1941. A large expansion of the Army Air Corps that was put in hand in February 1940 led to the arrival of the 32nd Pursuit Group in the Canal Zone early in 1941, also with P-36s on strength, while two other new Groups forming in the USA, the 35th and 36th, received P-36s for initial working up as they became available from the front line squadrons that were in process of converting to P-40s.

Early in 1941, the 18th Pursuit Squadron was detached from the 35th PG and sent to Alaska as the first air defence force stationed in that territory, serving as part of the 28th Composite Group. Twenty P-36As arrived in crates on 20 February 1941 and the squadron established its HQ at Elmendorf Field, Anchorage and also operated from Ladd Field, Fairbanks. The harsh Arctic conditions and inexperience of ground and air crews in this environment took a heavy toll of the aircraft, only nine remaining serviceable by August 1941. Re-equipment with P-40s began before the end of 1941 and there is no record of the P-36s flying in combat

The P-36C, depicted here in 1941 finish and with the cockpit open, could be distinguished from earlier USAAC versions of the Hawk 75 by the wing machine guns with external link collection boxes.

(Above left) The fourth production P-36A after conversion to XP-42 for use as a test-bed into engine cooling techniques using a closely-cowled Twin Wasp. (Above right) The XP-36F, one of the armament experiments conducted on P-36A airframes, with a 23-mm Madsen cannon in a fairing beneath each wing. (Below right) The line drawings depict (1), the Curtiss Model 75; (2), the same aircraft converted to Model 75B; (3), the Hawk 75A-4 and (4), three views of the P-36A with P-36C wing guns shown dotted.

against Japanese forces that attacked Alaskan targets in June 1942, by which time the Alaskan defences had been reinforced by the arrival of the 11th Fighter Squadron, also flying P-40s.

By the end of 1941, a total of 39 P-36s was available in the Hawaiian Islands, principally at Wheeler Field in the hands of the 46th and 47th Pursuit Squadrons. The four aircraft of the former unit that succeeded in getting airborne approximately one hour after the first wave of Japanese bombers struck were piloted by Lts Gordon H Sterling, Lewis M Sanders, J M Thacker and P Rasmussen. Sterling was quickly shot down but Sanders and Rasmussen each claimed the destruction of a Nakajima B5N1, these being, as already noted, the first Army Air Force victories of World War II. Of the few P-36s of the 47th PS that got airborne from the satellite field at Haliewa, one was shot down by American ground defences and none made contact with the enemy. Only 16 P-36As remained serviceable in Hawaii by the end of the Pearl Harbor attack but this figure increased to 27 by the end of the month. However, the Curtiss fighter saw no further combat with the USAAF.

One other variant was designated by the USAAF, this being the P-36G. A total of 30 P-36Gs was acquired in mid 1941, these being export Hawk 75A-8s ordered by Norway but undelivered at the time that nation was invaded by Germany. Powered by the Wright Cyclone R-1820-G5 engine, they were purchased by the USAAF in two batches (as noted later in this account) and were supplied during 1942/43 under Lend-Lease provisions to the *Cuerpo de Aeronautica del Peru* (CAP). Also in 1942, Brazil received 10 P-36As from the USAAF, presumably through Lend-Lease. These were all used aircraft, delivered to the *Fôrça Aérea Brasileira* on 8 March 1942 and used for approximately two years as advanced trainers at Natal and Recife.

Hawks for China, Argentina, Thailand

While the original Model 75 was still being evaluated by the Army Air Corps, Curtiss began to investigate the export potential of its new fighter. It was tacitly assumed that a version of the Army's P-36 would in due course become available for export — as proved to be the case — but there also appeared to be a market for a

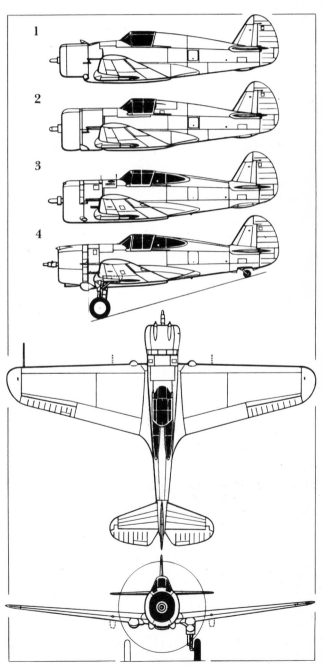

Registered NR1276, the Hawk 75-H demonstrator, with fixed landing gear, is shown here in Chinese insignia, as sold to China for the personal use of General Claire Chennault.

cheaper and somewhat less complex version of the Model 75 among some of the customers already using Hawk biplane fighters. To meet this need, the company put in hand, late in 1936, two new demonstrators with fixed landing gear and the Wright Cyclone GR-1820-G3 engine, rated at 875 hp for take-off and 840 hp at 8,700 ft (2 650 m). Known as Hawk 75s for export purposes, these demonstrators were Curtiss Model 75-H in the company's internal designating system, and differed from each other in small details. Curtiss offered, in these export models, the same two-gun installation in the upper front fuselage that had been designed from the outset for the Model 75, and also developed a centreline bomb rack with a 500-lb (227-kg) capacity and wing bomb racks that could carry ten 30-lb (13,6 kg) or six 50-lb (22,7-kg) bombs. The main undercarriage legs were faired by wide-chord trousers and the wheels had half-spats; the tailwheel was fixed.

A Cyclone-engined Hawk 75A-5 assembled by Hindustan Aircraft Ltd at Bangalore — one of only five examples completed in India before the programme was abandoned as over-ambitious.

The two demonstrators carried civil registrations NR 1276 and NR 1277 and the Chinese National Government was an early target for the Curtiss sales team. Curtiss already had close links with the Central Aircraft Manufacturing Company which was assembling Hawk III biplanes at Heng-Chow-Fu and a contract was soon secured for the supply of 30 similar Hawk 75-Ms powered by the Cyclone engine and with four 0.30-in (7,62-mm) guns, two in the fuselage and one in each wing. The original Hawk 75-H demonstrator NR 1276 was also purchased by China — on the personal account of Madame Chiang Kai-shek — and presented to General Claire L Chennault, who had been engaged to reorganize the Chinese air arm. One other Hawk supplied to China by Curtiss was listed as a Model 75-Q, delivered in November 1938, but its special features are not known.

The 30 Hawk 75-Ms were delivered between May and August 1938, and at the same time plans went ahead for the production of the Hawk 75 by CAMC at a new factory at Loi-Wing. The version involved was the Hawk 75A-5, this being an export model of the P-36A with retractable undercarriage, six 0.30-in (7,62-mm) machine guns (two in the fuselage and two in each wing) and a Wright GR-1820-G205A Cyclone engine. Only a few examples of the Hawk 75A-5 were completed and delivered from Loi-Wing before that factory was severely damaged by a Japanese bombing raid on 26 October 1940 and put out of action; according to some reports, however, up to 60 examples of the fixed-gear Model 75-M were also assembled in China from parts supplied by Curtiss. The Hawk 75A-5s went into service with the Chinese Air Force at Kunming during 1942, and some were also being flown by pilots of the AVG "Flying Tigers" for a short time before the Group disbanded in mid-1942.

A few months before the Loi-Wing factory was bombed, the government of India had taken the first steps to establish an aircraft industry and, by a chain of coincidences, a leading part in this venture had been played by William D Pawley, an American entrepreneur who had been largely responsible for the founding of CAMC in China. Consequently, when the latter company was forced to cease its production of the Hawk 75A-5, Pawley suggested that the surviving tools and assemblies should be transferred to Bangalore, where Hindustan Aircraft Ltd was establishing its factory. The Indian government agreed to the proposal, placing an order for 48 Hawk 75A-5s for its own use, and the first of these flew on 31 July 1942. However, HAL's over-ambitious production plans had to be scaled down and only five Hawks were completed in India, these entering service with the RAF as described later.

In Chinese hands, the Hawk 75-Ms appear to have achieved little success, suffering poor serviceability because of the lack of trained mechanics and a poor combat record because of low pilot proficiency. According to one report, six Hawks of a formation of 13 were written off in a Japanese attack on the training centre at Heng-yang. According to Chennault's own record of his period in China, three squadrons were equipped with Hawk 75-Ms.

While China was acquiring its Hawk 75s, the second 75-H demonstrator had aroused the interest of the Argentine government, which purchased this aircraft in June 1937 whilst placing an order for 29 similar Hawk 75-Os and acquiring a licence for production of the type at Cordoba. Featuring wider main wheel fairings than the 75-H, the Hawk 75-O also had the six-

(Above) One of the Hawk 75-Ns purchased by the Thai Air Force in 1938 and used briefly in operations against the Armée de l'Air *in 1941. (Right) The Hawk 75-Os acquired by the Argentine Air Force in 1938 were similar to the Thai Hawk 75-Ns in most respects but had an armament. of six Madsen 0.30-in (7,62-mm) machine guns.*

Curtiss Hawk 75-O Specification

Power Plant: One Wright GR-1820-G3 Cyclone nine-cylinder single-row air-cooled radial engine rated at 875 hp at 2,200 rpm for take-off and 840 hp at 2,100 rpm at 8,700 ft (2 654 m). Three bladed constant speed fully feathering propeller. Fuel capacity 107 US gal (405 l) in two wing tanks.
Performance: Max speed, 239 mph (384 km/h) at sea level and 280 mph (451 km/h) at 10,700 ft (3 260 m); normal cruising speed, 240 mph (386 km/h) at 10,700 ft (3 260 m); initial rate of climb, 2,340 ft/min (11,90 m/sec); time to 23,000 ft (7 010 m), 12.5 min; service ceiling, 31,800 ft (9 690 m); normal range, 547 mls (880 km); max range, 1,210 mls (1 947 km).
Weights: Empty, 3,975 lb (1 803 kg); normal loaded, 5,300 lb (2 400 kg); max gross, 6,418 lb (2 911 kg).
Dimensions: Span, 37 ft 4 in (11,39 m); length, 28 ft 7 in (8,72 m); height, 9 ft 3 in (2,82 m); wing area, 236 sq ft (21,92 m²); undercarriage track, 7 ft 3 in (2,20 m).
Armament: Two 0.30-in (7,62-mm) Madsen M.1935 machine guns in upper front fuselage and one similar gun in each wing. Provision under wings for A-3 bomb racks carrying ten 30-lb (13,6-kg) or six 50-lb (22,7-kg) bombs, and provision for one 500-lb (227-kg) bomb under fuselage.

gun armament (Madsen M.1935 guns of 0.30-in/7,62-mm calibre being used in all positions) and a revised exhaust system for the Cyclone GR-1820-G3 engine, with a semi-circle of electrically-operated gills at the rear of the cowling. The Curtiss-built 75-Os were delivered in November and December 1938 and were followed by 20 examples built by the Fabrica Militar, the first of which was delivered on 16 September 1940.

The Hawk 75-Os equipped the I, II and III *Regimientos de Caza*, and 45 were still in the inventory of the I and II *Regimientos* in 1945; the last examples were retired from front line service with the II *Regimiento* as late as 1953, and the Hawks flew for at least another year as advanced trainers at the *Escuela de Aviacion Militar* at Cordoba, vying with the Peruvian P-36Gs for a record of longevity.

One other nation purchased the fixed-gear version of the Hawk 75, this being Thailand. An order for 25 Hawk 75-Ns was placed by the Thai government, these having the Cyclone engine and wide-chord main leg fairings, two 7.9-mm machine guns in the fuselage and

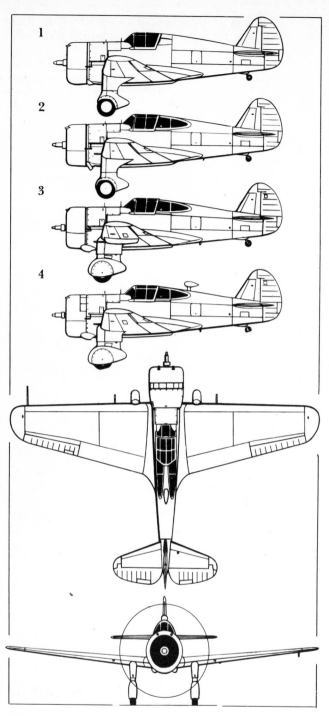

The side views in the above drawing depict (1), the Hawk 75 prototype with fixed undercarriage; (2), the Hawk 75-M and (3), the Hawk 75-N. The three-view (4) illustrates the Hawk 75-O.

a 23-mm Danish Madsen cannon in a fairing under each wing. Twelve 75-Ns were delivered in November and December 1938 but it is believed that the second batch of 13 was not completed.

The Thai Hawk 75-Ns saw brief action in January 1941 when Thai forces invaded French Indo China. Four Hawk 75-Ns each carrying 33-lb (15-kg) bombs, in company with nine Mitsubishi Ki.21-I bombers

attacking Nakorn Wat on 11 January, were intercepted by French Morane-Saulnier 406s, and two of the Hawk pilots each claimed the destruction of an MS 406, although these claims were refuted by *l'Armee de l'Air*. Equipping the 5th Wing of the Royal Thai Air Force at Prachuab Kirikhand, the Hawk 75-Ns saw action again on 7 December 1941, this time against Japanese forces invading Thailand. On this occasion, one third of the unit's serviceable fighters were lost during the brief but bitter fighting that took place before a ceasefire was agreed.

Hawks for France

In addition to its development of the fixed-gear Hawk 75-H, Curtiss naturally offered an export version of the basic P-36 as soon as it was permitted to do so by the US government. This export model wa designated the Hawk 75A, a series of sub-variants being further identified by suffix numbers. Thus, the Hawks 75A-1, A-2, A-3 and A-4 were all for France, the 75A-5 was the version licence-built in India, the 75A-6 and A-8 were ordered by Norway, the A-7 by the Netherlands East Indies and the A-9 by Iran. Further reference to the Norwegian, Netherlands and Iranian orders is made later.

French interest in the Hawk 75 began to emerge early in 1938, before the first P-36As had been delivered to US Army Air Corps, and in the face of Army disapproval, based on the latter's belief that Curtiss could not possibly meet its P-36A delivery schedules and in addition undertake the production of up to 30 a month for France from March 1939 onwards, as the company was offering. In urgent need of modern fighters in large numbers to try to match the pace of German rearmament, the *Armée de l'Air* persisted with the negotiations, despite a unit price of Fr 2,365,000 quoted by Curtiss for the Hawk 75A — almost double the going price for the French-built Morane-Saulnier 406 and Bloch MB-150 fighters of generally similar configuration and performance.

French interest in the Curtiss fighter was heightened after Michel Detroyat, one of the nation's leading test pilots, had been allowed to fly a Y1P-36 at Wright Field in March 1938, and submitted a thoroughly enthusiastic report. Politically, the high price remained an obstacle but when a report on the production programme for the MB-150 indicated that a complete structural redesign was required to suit that aircraft to mass production techniques, purchase of the Hawk 75A in large quantities was finally approved by the French government, and a purchasing mission was despatched to the USA with instructions to order 100 Hawk 75A-1 airframes and 175 Pratt & Whitney R-1830 engines. To speed production, the French government also agreed to finance additional machine tools and jigs, specifying in return that the first of the French Hawks should fly by 25 November 1938 and the 100th should be delivered by 10 April 1939. It was also implicit in the negotiations that additional French orders would follow if all went well with initial production.

The Hawk 75A-1 ordered by France was powered by an R-1830-SC-G Twin Wasp with an international rating of 900 hp at 12,000 ft (3 657 m) and 950 hp for take-off. Fuel capacity comprised 135 Imp gal (613 l) in four tanks in the fuselage and the armament consisted of four 7,5-mm FN-Browning Mle 38 machine guns, two in the front upper fuselage with 600 rpg and one in each wing with 500 rpg. All instruments except the altimeter were metric calibrated, the throttle was modified to work in the customary French sense, which was the reverse of American and British practice, and a modified seat was introduced to accommodate the French Lemercier back-parachute. French equipment included a Baille-Lemaire gun sight, a Radio-Industrie 537 radio and a Munerelle oxygen system.

The first two Hawk 75A-1s were completed and flown at Buffalo early in December 1938, within a few days of the contractual date and after acceptance tests by a resident French pilot, deliveries to France began with the arrival at Le Havre of the fourth and fifth aircraft on 24 December in the SS *Paris*. Erected at Le Havre, these Hawk 75A-1s were flown to Bourges, where the Societe Nationale de Construction Aeronautiques du Centre (SNCAC) had been given responsibility for assembly of the Curtiss fighters. The delivery rate built up rapidly, with 14 more completed aircraft supplied in January 1939 and the first SNCAC-assembled Hawk following in February. By 12 May, all 100 aircraft of the first contract were in service, the first units to convert (from Dewoitine 500/501 fighters) being *Groupes de Chasse* I/4 and II/4 of the 4e *Escadre de Chasse* and GC I/5 of the 5e *Escadre*, at Reims.

An option on a second batch of 100 Hawks was taken up by *l'Armée de l'Air* on 8 March 1939, with an order for 150 more R-1830s being placed at the same time. Provision was made in these aircraft for an additional FN-Browning machine gun in each wing; some structural reinforcement was made of the rear fuselage and provision was made for interchangeability between the SC-G engine and the more powerful R-1830-SC3-G

with a rating of 1,050 hp for take-off. With these modifications, the aircraft was designated Hawk 75A-2 by Curtiss.

The first examples of the Hawk 75A-2 reached Le Havre at the end of May 1939. Thirty-two Hawk 75A-2s were accepted by the *Armée de l'Air* during July, 36 in August and 29 during September. The uprated SC3-G engine was first tested, at the *Centre d'Essais du Materiel Aerien*, in the 20th Hawk 75A-2 but this engine was only introduced as standard with the 41st A-2, which was also the first to have the increased armament.

By the time war broke out in Europe, Hawk 75As were in the hands of a fourth *Groupe de Chasse*, the newly-formed GC II/4, each *Groupe* having a theoretical strength of 18 aircraft but in fact possessing up to 25 aircraft; many more were in the pipeline, all 200 75A-1s and A-2s having been delivered by Curtiss by September 1939. Under a new operational organization introduced by *l'Armée de l'Air* as soon as the war started, GC I/4 and I/5 becoming part of *Groupement* 23 and II/4 and II/5 becoming part of GP 22. These *Groupements* were responsible, in order of priority, for the protection of airfields and strategic railways, and the interception of enemy aircraft returning from long-range intrusions over France. In addition, the fighter units could be assigned to Land Armies Command for observation and reconnaissance duties, and the Hawk 75 units were frequently so used in 1939/40.

(Above right) A Hawk 75A-3 — the Twin Wasp engine indicated by the long-chord cowling — of the 2e Escadrille, GC/5, serving with the Armée de l'Air in 1939. (Below) The French Groupe de Chasse I/5 was one of the first units to equip with the Curtiss Hawk; this example bears the insignia of both escadrilles of the Groupe and is flown by the CO or Adjutant of the unit.

Curtiss Hawk 75A-4 (Mohawk IV) Cutaway Drawing Key

1 Starboard navigation light
2 Starboard aileron
3 Aileron tab
4 Aileron ball and socket control linkage
5 Access plate
6 Wing skinning
7 Fuselage machine gun blast tubes
8 Machine gun muzzle fairings

39 Pilot's headrest/back armour
40 Sutton harness
41 Pilot's seat
42 Elevator control
43 Seat support frame
44 Angled fuselage frame
45 Fuselage fuel tank, capacity 47.8 Imp gal (217 l)
46 Entry handhold
47 Canopy track
48 Fuel filler cap/neck
49 Expansion tank
50 Rear-view glazing/cut-out

The *Groupes* flying Hawk 75As were quickly in action patrolling over the Siegfried and Maginot lines, and it was on such a mission that aircraft of GC II/4 shot down two Bf 109s to score the first aerial victories of World War II. By the end of September, the *Armée de l'Air* claimed the destruction of 37 German aircraft, most of which fell to the guns of the Hawks, but this period of the *Drole de Guerre* was one of only small-scale and sporadic action and it was not until the Battle for France began on 10 May 1940 that the Hawk units were fully extended. By this time, GC I/4 had become part of a new *Groupement* 25 responsible for the defence of Northern France and a start had been made

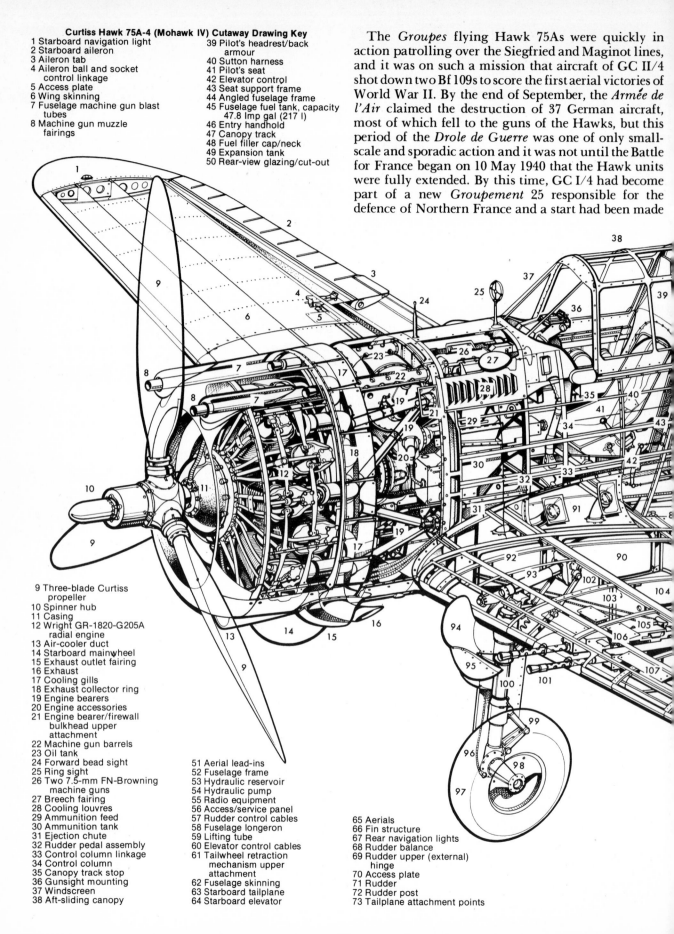

9 Three-blade Curtiss propeller
10 Spinner hub
11 Casing
12 Wright GR-1820-G205A radial engine
13 Air-cooler duct
14 Starboard mainwheel
15 Exhaust outlet fairing
16 Exhaust
17 Cooling gills
18 Exhaust collector ring
19 Engine bearers
20 Engine accessories
21 Engine bearer/firewall bulkhead upper attachment
22 Machine gun barrels
23 Oil tank
24 Forward bead sight
25 Ring sight
26 Two 7.5-mm FN-Browning machine guns
27 Breech fairing
28 Cooling louvres
29 Ammunition feed
30 Ammunition tank
31 Ejection chute
32 Rudder pedal assembly
33 Control column linkage
34 Control column
35 Canopy track stop
36 Gunsight mounting
37 Windscreen
38 Aft-sliding canopy

51 Aerial lead-ins
52 Fuselage frame
53 Hydraulic reservoir
54 Hydraulic pump
55 Radio equipment
56 Access/service panel
57 Rudder control cables
58 Fuselage longeron
59 Lifting tube
60 Elevator control cables
61 Tailwheel retraction mechanism upper attachment
62 Fuselage skinning
63 Starboard tailplane
64 Starboard elevator

65 Aerials
66 Fin structure
67 Rear navigation lights
68 Rudder balance
69 Rudder upper (external) hinge
70 Access plate
71 Rudder
72 Rudder post
73 Tailplane attachment points

38

on the conversion of GC III/2 to Hawk 75As at Chartres.

Between 10 May and 24 June, when France capitulated, the Hawk 75As saw intensive action, being responsible for the destruction of one third of all enemy aircraft claimed by *l'Armée de l'Air* up to that date, although they represented considerably less than one-third of the fighter strength. Of 11 French pilots

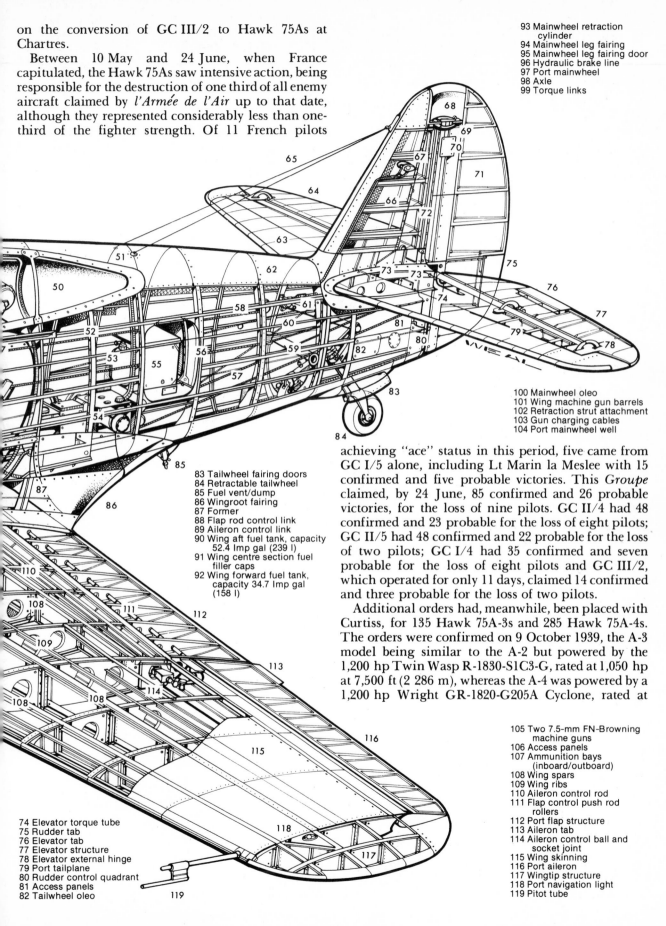

achieving "ace" status in this period, five came from GC I/5 alone, including Lt Marin la Meslee with 15 confirmed and five probable victories. This *Groupe* claimed, by 24 June, 85 confirmed and 26 probable victories, for the loss of nine pilots. GC II/4 had 48 confirmed and 23 probable for the loss of eight pilots; GC II/5 had 48 confirmed and 22 probable for the loss of two pilots; GC I/4 had 35 confirmed and seven probable for the loss of eight pilots and GC III/2, which operated for only 11 days, claimed 14 confirmed and three probable for the loss of two pilots.

Additional orders had, meanwhile, been placed with Curtiss, for 135 Hawk 75A-3s and 285 Hawk 75A-4s. The orders were confirmed on 9 October 1939, the A-3 model being similar to the A-2 but powered by the 1,200 hp Twin Wasp R-1830-S1C3-G, rated at 1,050 hp at 7,500 ft (2 286 m), whereas the A-4 was powered by a 1,200 hp Wright GR-1820-G205A Cyclone, rated at

1,000 hp at 15,000 ft (4 570 m). The first 50 Hawk 75A-3s were modified to permit the installation of Colt MG 40 machine guns in place of the FN-Brownings, these weapons being bored to the same 7,5-mm calibre to accept the French M29 cartridges. With a normal weight of 5,732 lb (2 600 kg) the Hawk 75A-3 climbed at 2,346 ft/min (11,92 m/sec) and had a maximum speed of 311 mph (500 km/h) at 10,000 ft (3 050 m), virtually the same as the P-36A. The Hawk 75A-4, on the other hand, at a weight of 5,750 lb (2 608 kg), proved to be the fastest production model of the basic fighter, the maximum speed being 323 mph (520 km/h), cruising speed 262 mph (422 km/h) and absolute range with overload fuel, 1,003 mls (1 614 km).

All Hawk 75A-3s were scheduled to be delivered to France between February and May 1940, and the first 12 reached Le Havre on 15 March. Acceptances did not keep pace with assembly at Bourges, because of delays in the delivery of some items of French equipment, and by the time France capitulated, only 110 had been *officially* taken on charge by *l'Armée de l'Air*, although in the last few days of the fighting, as *Wehrmacht* forces approached Bourges, some Hawk 75A-3s were flown out by service pilots less some operational equipment and without the formality of official acceptance. All but two of the A-3s had been shipped by Curtiss by early May 1940, the others being retained for test and development flying.

The Hawk 75A-4s followed immediately after the A-3s, a production rate of two a day being achieved by Curtiss, but only six had been officially taken on strength by *l'Armée de l'Air* at the time of the Armistice; 30 more were being unloaded at La Rochelle in June when the vessel carrying them sank, another 17 were disembarked at Martinique and six at Guadaloupe, leaving over 100 in the USA still to be delivered. These, as related later, were taken over by Britain as Mohawk IVs, whilst some of the A-4s already in France fell into German hands and ended up in service with the Finnish Air Force.

Hawk 75A-3s were assigned as replacement aircraft to the various *Groupes de Chasse* but the handful of A-4s, despite their potentially improved performance, proved thoroughly unreliable because of the Cyclone engine installation. Shortly before the end of fighting in

A Hawk 75A-2 of GC II/4, one of the Armée de l'Air *units heavily involved in the air fighting over France in the spring of 1940.*

France, all the Hawk-equipped units were ordered to fly their aircraft to North Africa, GC I/4 and GC III/2 crossing the Mediterranean on 18 June, GC II/4 on the 19th and GC I/5 and GC II/5 on the 20th. GC II/4 and III/2 were disbanded on 25 August 1940 in North Africa, but the other three units continued to fly the Hawk 75As, GC I/5 at Rabat, GC II/5 at Casablanca and GC I/4 at Dakar. When British naval forces attacked the French fleet at Mers-el-Kebir on 3 July 1940 to prevent it falling into German hands, Hawk 75As of GC I/5 and II/5 defended the port and shot down several Fleet Air Arm Blackburn Skuas.

More than a year later, the same Hawk *Groupes* again went into action against Allied forces, when the Operation Torch invasion of North Africa began on 8 November 1942. In a single day, intense fighting occurred between the Hawks and US Navy F4F Wildcats, in which 15 of the Curtiss fighters were destroyed, with eight pilots killed, and at least seven Wildcats fell to French guns. This effectively ended the operational career of the Hawk 75A in French service; the surviving aircraft were relegated to a training rôle at Meknes where they were joined, in 1943, by some of the Hawk 75A-4s recovered from Martinique and Guadeloupe, where they had been standing in the open air for more than two years. In the training rôle in Morocco, the Hawk 75A-4s proved thoroughly unreliable, primarily because of an unsatisfactory oil feed system, and during 1944 Twin Wasps were fitted in place of the Cyclone engines. Between 1944 and 1946, all the surviving French Hawk 75As were used at the flying training school at Kasbah-Tadla, where they were the first single-seaters flown by pupils; they were then transferred to Cazaux to be used, until 1950, as aerial gunnery targets.

Britain's Mohawks

Upon the collapse of organised resistance in France, arrangements were hurriedly made for outstanding French aircraft contracts in the USA to be taken over by Britain. So far as the Curtiss Hawk was concerned, this involved the balance of approximately 115 Hawk 75A-4s already in production, to which appear to have been added a further batch of 110 on which France had taken an option. RAF serial number allocations are known for a total of 224 ex-French Hawks (in the serial ranges AR, AX, BB, BJ, BK, BL, BS and BT).

For service with the RAF, the Hawk 75A was given the name Mohawk, and mark numbers were allocated to the A-1, A-2, A-3 and A-4 versions, which became the Mohawk I, II, III and IV respectively. This action was taken when it appeared that some of the earlier French aircraft might be flown across the Channel to Britain in June 1940; although a number of French aircraft *did* arrive in this way, there is no record of the number of Hawks that they included; a few Mohawk IIIs served with the RAF but the great majority were Hawk 75A-4s received direct from the USA.

The Curtiss fighter was by no means an unknown quantity to the RAF, for as early as November 1939 a

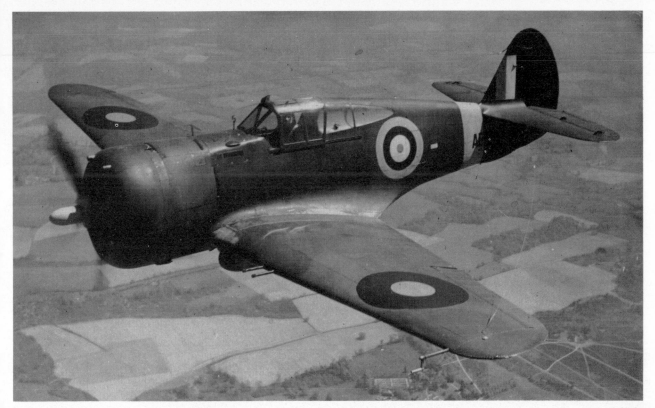

(Above) A number of Hawk 75s diverted from French contracts and others that escaped from France entered service with the RAF as Mohawks; this example is a Hawk 75A-4 as shown by the short-chord engine cowling. (Below) A Mohawk III with Twin Wasp engine and fairings over the cowling gun-ports.

Hawk 75A-1 had been flown (in France) by Sqn Ldr J F X McKenna on behalf of the A and AEE. His report had said that the Hawk was "exceptionally easy and pleasant to fly, the aileron control being particularly powerful" and that it was "more manoeuvrable at high speed than the Hurricane or the Spitfire". This report naturally aroused considerable interest in official circles in Britain, and as a result arrangements were made for a Hawk 75 to be borrowed from *l'Armée de l'Air* for further evaluation in Britain. The 88th Hawk 75A-2 was used, in consequence, at the RAE from 29 December 1939 to 13 January 1940 for a 12-hr flight programme covering handling in general, and specifically by comparison with the Spitfire, Hurricane and Gloster F.5/34; mock combats were staged between the Hawk and a production Spitfire I (K9944), fitted with the early two-pitch propeller.

The Hawk 75A-2 was flown with aft tank empty at a loaded weight of 6,025 lb (2 733 kg) and the three RAF pilots participating in the evaluation were unanimous in their praise for the US fighter's exceptional handling characteristics and beautifully harmonised controls. In a diving attack at 400 mph (644 km/h), the Hawk was far superior to the Spitfire, thanks to its lighter ailerons, and in a dogfight at 250 mph (402 km/h) the Hawk was again the superior machine because its elevator control was not over-sensitive and all-round view was better; but the Spitfire could break off combat at will because of its very much higher maximum speed. In a dive at 400 mph (644 km/h), the Spitfire pilot, exerting all his

Curtiss Hawk 75A-4 Specification

Power Plant: One Wright GR-1820-G205A Cyclone nine-cylinder single-row radial air cooled engine rated at 1,200 hp for take-off and at 4,200 ft (1 280 m) and 1,000 hp at 15,000 ft (4 570 m). Fuel capacity, 105 US gal (397 l) in two wing tanks and 57 US gal (217 l) in optional fuselage tank.

Performance: Max speed, 323 mph (520 km/h) at 15,100 ft (4 877 m) and 272 mph (438 km/h) at sea level; typical cruising speed, 262 mph (422 km/h) at 10,000 ft (3 050 m); initial rate of climb, 2,820 ft/min (14,32 m/sec); service ceiling, 32,700 ft (9 967 m); normal range 670 mls (1 078 km); max range (with overload fuel), 1,010 mls (1 625 km).

Weights: Empty equipped, 4,541 lb (2 060 kg); normal loaded, 5,750 lb (2 608 kg).

Dimensions: Span, 37 ft 4 in (11,38 m); length, 28 ft 7¾ in (8,74 m); height, 9 ft 3 in (2,82 m); wing area, 236 sq ft (21,92 m²); dihedral, 6 deg constant; undercarriage track, 8 ft 0⅞ in (2,46 m).

Armament: Two 7,5-mm FN-Browning Mle 38 machine guns with 600 rpg in upper front fuselage and two similar guns in each wing with 500 rpg.

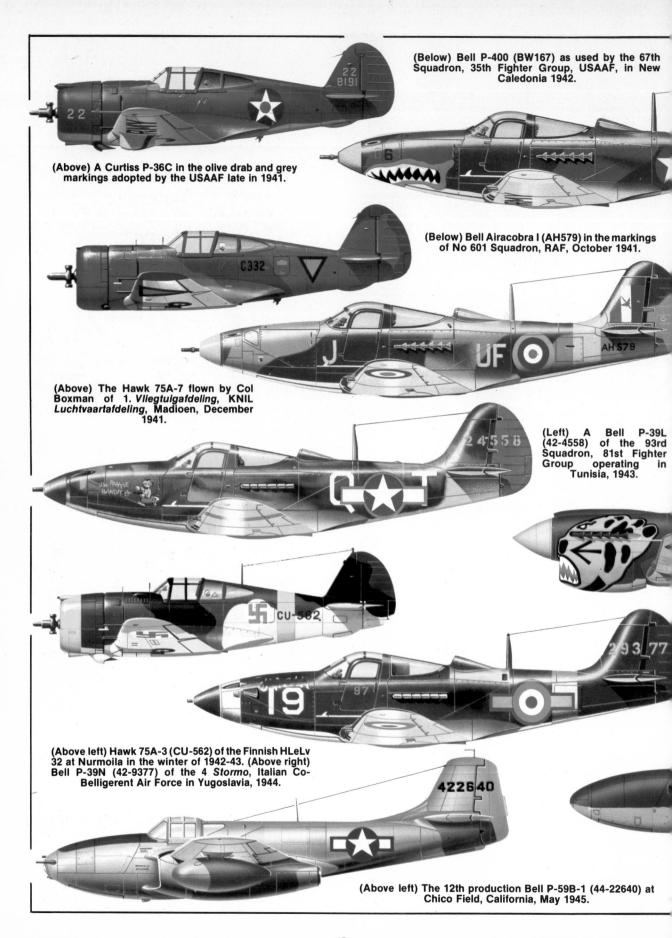

(Above) A Curtiss P-36C in the olive drab and grey markings adopted by the USAAF late in 1941.

(Below) Bell P-400 (BW167) as used by the 67th Squadron, 35th Fighter Group, USAAF, in New Caledonia 1942.

(Above) The Hawk 75A-7 flown by Col Boxman of 1. *Vliegtuigafdeling*, KNIL *Luchtvaartafdeling*, Madioen, December 1941.

(Below) Bell Airacobra I (AH579) in the markings of No 601 Squadron, RAF, October 1941.

(Left) A Bell P-39L (42-4558) of the 93rd Squadron, 81st Fighter Group operating in Tunisia, 1943.

(Above left) Hawk 75A-3 (CU-562) of the Finnish HLeLv 32 at Nurmoila in the winter of 1942-43. (Above right) Bell P-39N (42-9377) of the 4 *Stormo*, Italian Co-Belligerent Air Force in Yugoslavia, 1944.

(Above left) The 12th production Bell P-59B-1 (44-22640) at Chico Field, California, May 1945.

42

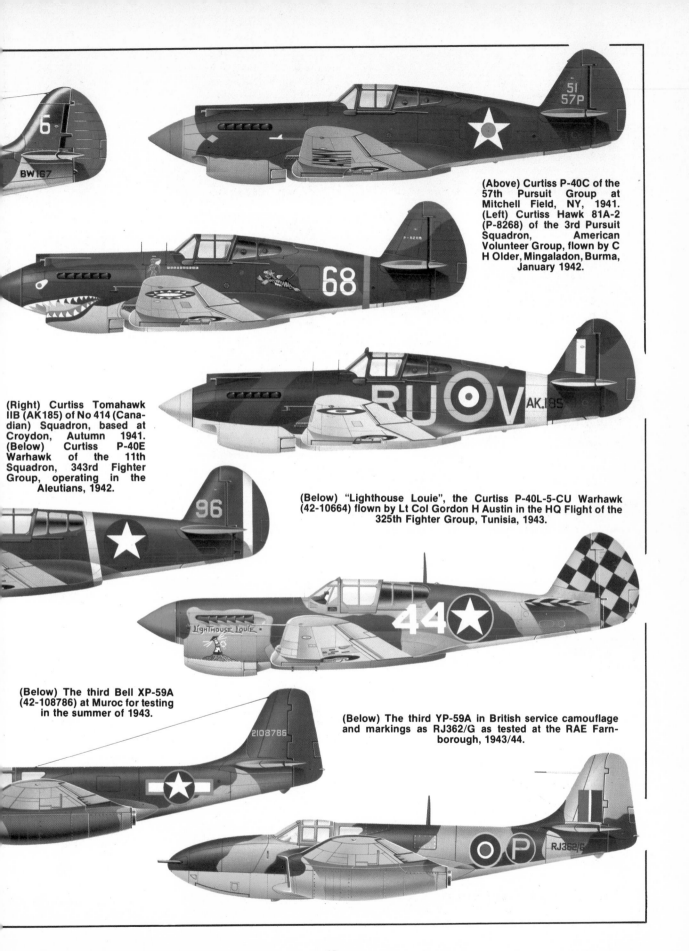

(Above) Curtiss P-40C of the 57th Pursuit Group at Mitchell Field, NY, 1941.
(Left) Curtiss Hawk 81A-2 (P-8268) of the 3rd Pursuit Squadron, American Volunteer Group, flown by C H Older, Mingaladon, Burma, January 1942.

(Right) Curtiss Tomahawk IIB (AK185) of No 414 (Canadian) Squadron, based at Croydon, Autumn 1941.
(Below) Curtiss P-40E Warhawk of the 11th Squadron, 343rd Fighter Group, operating in the Aleutians, 1942.

(Below) "Lighthouse Louie", the Curtiss P-40L-5-CU Warhawk (42-10664) flown by Lt Col Gordon H Austin in the HQ Flight of the 325th Fighter Group, Tunisia, 1943.

(Below) The third Bell XP-59A (42-108786) at Muroc for testing in the summer of 1943.

(Below) The third YP-59A in British service camouflage and markings as RJ362/G as tested at the RAE Farnborough, 1943/44.

(Above) One of ten Hawk 75A-9s built for Iran, photographed in the USA before delivery; they were captured by the RAF before being assembled in Iran. (Below) A Mohawk IV receives pre-flight attention from pilot and ground crew.

strength, could apply no more than one-fifth aileron because of high stick forces whereas the Curtiss pilot could apply three-quarter aileron.

When the Spitfire dived on the Hawk, both aircraft travelling at 350-400 mph (560-645 km/h), the Curtiss fighter's pilot could avoid his opponent by applying its ailerons quickly, banking and turning rapidly. The Spitfire could not follow the Hawk round in this manoeuvre and consequently overshot the target. In the reverse situation, however, the Hawk could easily follow the Spitfire until the latter's superior speed allowed it to pull away. The superior manoeuvrability of the Hawk was ascribed mainly to the over-sensitiveness of the Spitfire's elevator, which resulted in some difficulty in accurately controlling the 'g' in a tight turn; over-correction held the risk of an inadvertent stall being induced.

Because of the difference in propellers, the Hawk displayed appreciably better take-off and climb characteristics. The swing on take-off was smaller and more easily corrected than on the British fighter and during the climb the Hawk's controls were more effective; but the Curtiss fighter proved to be rather slow in picking up speed in a dive, making the Spitfire the more suitable machine of the two for intercepting high-speed bombers (which was, of course, the primary rôle for which the British aircraft had been designed).

Notwithstanding the excellence of this report on the Hawk 75A-2's handling, the RAF found little use for the Mohawks that began to arrive in Britain a few months later. Upon arrival, they were modified to have British throttle movement, six Browning 0,303-in

(7,7-mm) machine guns, British gun sight, instrumentation and radio and standard RAF day fighter finish. Apart from one or two assigned to the A & AEE Boscombe Down for the preparation of handling notes, they were then despatched to various MUs for storage until an operational need arose for their use. In fact, they saw no combat service in the UK, and from the end of 1940 onwards, most of the Mohawk IVs were shipped to South Africa (for use by the SAAF) and to India (for use by the RAF). At least 72 Mohawks reached South Africa during 1941 and at the end of 1942 there were 74 in India; in addition, Britain supplied 12 Mohawk IVs to Portugal in October 1941 after that nation had invoked the Anglo-Portuguese Treaty of Military Alliance and requested fighter aircraft to reinforce the *Arma da Aeronautica*. These aircraft entered service at Ota, in a unit later known as the *Esquadrilha* XY; subsequently, they were transferred to São Miguel to provide the defence of the Azores.

The first Mohawk for South Africa arrived at Takoradi (Gold Coast, now Ghana) at the end of 1940 but crashed into the sea on its first flight there, on 27 December. Further deliveries were delayed to allow modifications to be made to the Cyclone engines and it was not until the East African campaign had ended that the first 20 Mohawks with modified engines became available, in July 1941. Three were issued to No 41 Squadron Fighter Detachment, and after training at Nairobi this unit moved with its Mohawks to Aiscia, Somalia, close to the border with the Vichy-French Somalia, becoming in October 1941, Flight B of No 3 Squadron. Operations were mounted against Italian targets at Gondar in Ethiopia, the Mohawks carrying bomb racks under the wings to attack ground targets and A Flight of No 3 Squadron receiving the Curtiss fighters also in this period.

No 4 Squadron, SAAF, worked up on Mohawks at Nakuru, Kenya, in 1941, but converted to P-40 Tomahawks before moving to the Middle East for operations, and a similar course was followed by No 5 Squadron, which trained on Mohawks at Germiston. No 7 Squadron similarly trained on the Curtiss fighter at Swartkop and then handed them on to No 6 Squadron in April 1942, this unit making operational use of the Mohawk in defence of the South African homeland, its duties including off-shore anti-shipping and anti-U-boat patrols. Similar duties were performed for a short period by No 10 Squadron, but Nos 6 and 10 were both dissolved in July 1943, after which Mohawks continued in use as advanced trainers at SAAF OTUs until the end of the war.

In India, the RAF's No 5 Squadron began to convert from Hawker Audax biplanes to the Mohawk IV at Dum Dum, Calcutta, in December 1941, and for a time this unit was destined to provide the sole fighter defence of NE India. In April 1942, No 146 Squadron also began to convert to the Mohawk, but this plan was changed and its aircraft were transferred to No 5 in April. The latter unit flew its first operational sortie with the Mohawk IV on 17 June 1942, subsequently engaging in bomber escort duties, standing patrols and

A number of French and Norwegian Hawk 75s captured by the Luftwaffe *were completely refurbished (this example was photographed in France) and were then sold to Finland.*

close-support attacks, claiming its first "kill" on 20 August. During January 1943, the first "rhubarbs" were flown on the Imphal and Chindwin rivers, and these became an important part of No 5 Squadron's operational activities until June, when the Mohawks were replaced by Hurricanes.

Meanwhile, No 155 Squadron had also become operational on the Mohawk IV, having formed at Peshawar on 1 April 1942 and becoming operational in September when it flew convoy patrols and scrambles in defence of Madras. Offensive missions began the following month with an attack on Shwebo and Japanese aircraft were encountered for the first time on 10 November, when two Mohawks were lost. In common with other users of the Cyclone-engined Mohawk IV, this unit suffered constant problems with the oil circulation systems, and the aircraft were grounded from time to time, but they were involved in heavy fighting at Imphal during February and March 1943, and in May they began dive-bombing attacks using 20-lb (9-kg) bombs, continuing to use Mohawks until the end of 1944.

In addition to the ex-French Mohawk IVs shipped out from the UK, the Indian squadrons took on

strength the five Hawk 75A-5s assembled by Hindustan Aircraft at Bangalore (identifiable by serial numbers in the LA series). Also, the 10 Hawk 75A-9s that had been ordered in 1940 by the Iranian Imperial Air Force are reported to have been shipped to India after they had been discovered, still in their crates, by the British forces that occupied Iran in August 1941. After assembly at Drigh Road, Karachi, these Cyclone-engined, six-gun aircraft are understood to have been issued to No 5 Squadron at Dum Dum, although no record of their RAF serial numbers appears to exist and they may have been used only as a source of spares.

Norwegian and Finnish Hawks

An order for 12 Hawk 75A-6s was placed with Curtiss in the autumn of 1939 by the Norwegian Army Flying Service (*Hærens Flyvevåben*), as part of a six-year expansion programme launched in 1938 with the object of enlarging the *Jagerbataljon* (Fighter Battalion) to three 12-aircraft *Jagervinger*. The version selected for Norwegian use had the Pratt & Whitney R-1830-SC3-G engines like the French 75A-2s, and a four-gun armament with 7,9-mm machine guns in the fuselage and wings. A licence for the production of another 24 Hawk 75A-6s was also obtained by Norway and plans were made for this work to be undertaken by the Army Aircraft Factory at Kjeller. However, when it became obvious that this plan would not allow the *Jager-bataljon* to be brought up to strength by the target date of 1 July 1940, a second batch of 12 Hawks was ordered from Curtiss (leaving one *Jagerving* to fly Gloster Gladiators).

With the deteriorating situation in Europe, the Norwegian government decided in January 1940 to double its fighter strength with formation of second *Jagerbataljon*, and placed an order for 36 Hawk 75A-8s, these having the GR-1820-G205A Cyclone engine and increased armament of two 12.7-mm guns in the fuselage and four in the wings. By the time the invasion

Hawk 75s acquired by Finland's Ilmavoimat *from Germany included A-1, A-2, A-3 and A-6 versions; illustrated is an A-3. The type was operated by LeLv 32 throughout the Continuation War.*

A batch of 36 Hawk 75A-8s ordered by Norway was completed too late to participate in the European air war but they operated in Norwegian markings as advanced trainers in Canada in 1940-43.

of Norway was launched, however, only four of the first batch of the Hawk 75A-6s had been assembled at Kjeller, and another eight were still in their shipping crates at Oslo harbour, where they were eventually captured by the German forces. The final disposition of the second batch of 12 Hawk 75A-6s is uncertain; some reports indicate that they were shipped from Curtiss but diverted while *en route* to France and eventually passed into service with the RAF. It is known, however, that at least 13 Hawk 75A-6s were eventually made airworthy and sold by Germany to Finland (as described later) suggesting that at least some of the second batch were captured also, possibly in France.

All 36 Hawk 75A-8s were still awaiting delivery when Norway fell, and towards the end of 1940 six were despatched to Canada for use as advanced trainers at the Little Norway flying training centre established at Island Airport, Toronto. The other 30 followed during the first two months of 1941, but the number of Hawks on hand was more than needed by the training school and on 5 May 1942 the USAAF agreed to purchase 18 of these aircraft for supply to Peru through Lend-Lease arrangements, when they received the designation P-36G. After full overhaul by Curtiss at Buffalo in July 1942, they were flown down to Peru, where they were destined to serve with the *Cuerpo de Aeronautica del Peru* until 1947. When the Norwegian operations at Island Airport were closed down early in 1943, 12 more Hawks were acquired by USAAF (making 30 P-36Gs in all) and 10 of these also went to Peru; the balance of six Hawk 75A-8s had been written off in Canada.

The Hawk 75A-6s captured by Germany in Oslo, plus more than 30 assorted French models, were in due course transported to Espenlaub Flugzeugbau at Wuppertal, where they were completely overhauled and fitted with German instrumentation, Revi C12/C reflector sights and FuG 7a radio. In the Spring of 1941, the *Luftwaffe* agreed to sell a number of these aircraft to

Finland's air arm, *Illmavoimat*, and an initial quantity of 16 Hawk 75s arrived between 23 and 30 June, 1941, just as Finland resumed hostilities against the Soviet Union. Included in this batch were seven Cyclone-engined Hawk 75A-4s, the remainder being Twin Wasp models — two A-2s, one A-3 and six ex-Norwegian A-6s. The aircraft received serial numbers with the CU prefix, in some cases a small C (Cyclone) or W (Twin Wasp) appearing as a suffix to these.

Between 28 July and 2 August another 11 Hawks arrived, of which seven were A-6s, two were A-1s and two were A-3s. Two more A-3s arrived on 5 December. All these aircraft, totalling 29, arrived in Finland in crates, being assembled by the State Aircraft Factory for delivery to the squadrons. Briefly, the Curtiss fighters were used by LeLv (*Lentolaivue*) 12 and LeLv 14, but these units passed their aircraft on to LeLv 32 on 14 July, receiving Fokker D.XXIs in their place. Based at Utti, LeLv 32 began operations immediately with a mixture of equipment including some Fokker D.XXIs, and the Hawks achieved their first success on 16 July 1941 when a flight intercepted four I-153s and shot one of these biplanes down.

Additional Hawk deliveries to LeLv 32 allowed the squadron to relinquish the last of its Fokkers, and by September, now based at Lappeeranta, the unit had claimed the destruction of 26 Soviet aircraft (I-153s, I-16s and MiGs) for the loss of two Hawks. In the last air fighting during the Soviet advance into the Karelian Peninsula, a flight of the Curtiss fighters shot down seven I-153s without loss and success of this order continued with interceptions of DB-3F bombers and MiG-3s, although the superior speed of the latter type allowed the Soviet pilots to break off the engagement at will. LeLv 32 began 1942 with 14 Curtiss fighters in service (the name Hawk was seldom if ever used by the Finns, who adopted the diminutive *Sussu* for the little fighters, which were regarded as being among the best available to *Illmavoimat*. On 28 March, the squadron mounted a 12-aircraft formation over Suuraari, which had just been occupied by Finnish troops, when 29 Soviet aircraft launched an attack; in the ensuing battle, 17 of the attackers were shot down and six damaged, again without loss.

In May 1942, LeLv 32 moved to Nurmoila in the Soviet Union, as the main fighter element of the newly formed *Lentorykmentti* (Flight Regiment) 1, losing a Curtiss en route. Fierce fighting over the Svir River took its toll during the summer of 1942, but LeLv 32 continued to score many victories, despite being opposed by more modern Soviet aircraft, among the types being shot down being LaGG-3s, Yak-1s, Pe-2s and MBR flying boats as well as I-16s and MiG-3s. By 13 March 1943, the unit's strength was down to eight Curtiss fighters (and a captured LaGG-3), and by 14 June five more of the Hawks had been lost. Consequently, arrangements were made to purchase a further 15 aircraft from the German War Booty Depot and the squadron's pilots were dispatched to ferry the first of these direct to Finland from Dusseldorf. Comprising another four Hawk 75A-1s, seven A-2s and four A-3s, they reached Finland over the next seven months — four in June 1943, five in July, two in September, one in November and three in January 1944.

By the end of January 1944, therefore, LeLv 32 had 18 Curtiss fighters at Nurmoila, being renamed *Havittajalentolaivue* (Fighter Squadron) 32, or HLeLv 32, on 14 February. Losses continued, with activities on a fairly small scale, but on 6 June a new Soviet Air Force type was encountered and shot down — this being a B-26 Marauder; an A-20 Boston was claimed on 4 July, and on 26 July the unit's last victory was a U-2 biplane, shot down in Naataoja. Following the armistice on 4 September, the squadron moved to Rantasalmi and then Mikkeli. It had claimed 190 victories in just over three years of action, for the loss of 24 out of 44 Curtiss Hawks supplied to Finland — eight in aerial combat, six by ack-ack, one by enemy bombing and nine in accidents; 16 pilots were killed and two became PoWs. The surviving aircraft were transferred to HLeLv 13 at the end of 1944 and then formed the equipment of HLeLv 11 until being finally phased out of service early in 1948; a few also flew at the LeSK flying shcool.

The Netherland Hawks

Shortly after the war started in Europe, the Royal Netherlands Indies Army Air Corps (*Militaire Luchtvaartafdeling van het Koninklijk Nederlands-Indisch Leger or ML-KNIL*) placed an order (in October 1939) for 20 Hawks 75A-7s, to be powered by the Cyclone GR-1820-G205A engine and having an armament of one 12,7-mm and one 7,7-mm in the fuselage and two 7,7-mm guns in the wings. These aircraft began to reach the East-Indies during 1941, where the 12,7-mm fuselage gun was replaced by a 7,7-mm weapon to standardise on ammunition. Like the *Armée de l'Air*, the ML-KNIL found the Cyclone engine extremely troublesome, particularly during inverted flight and aerobatics. When the war with Japan began on 8 December 1941, 16 Hawk 75A-7s were airworthy, of which 12 were on the strength of 1.*Vliegtuigafdeling* of the 4e *Vliegtuiggroep* at Madioen. On 21 December, four Hawks of this unit took off to attack a rail junction with 50-lb (22,7-kg) bombs carried on underwing racks, but two collided on take-off and one was shot down during the attack. Only limited action was seen by the unit during ensuing weeks, but the strength of 1.VLG IV was down to eight aircraft by 3 February 1942, when the entire squadron took off to intercept the first Japanese bombing raid on Java. Two returned with engine trouble, four were diverted to intercept an incoming raid on Surabaya, three of these being shot down by Zero-Sens, and the other two claimed the destruction of at least one of the bombers in the original formation. However, the last two Hawk 75A-7s still airworthy on 5 February were shot down in a further engagement and the fighting career of the ML-KNIL Hawks was at an end.

Hawk 75A-7s of the Royal Netherlands Indies Army Air Corps in formation over Java. They saw brief but vicious action against Japanese forces invading the East Indies in 1941.

CURTISS HAWK 81A (P-40 AND TOMAHAWK)

The Curtiss Aeroplane Division of Curtiss-Wright having succeeded in its first attempt to produce a monoplane fighter — the Hawk 75 family previously described — the company was naturally looking, within a very short period of time, towards the development of fighters of improved performance in order to maintain its competitive advantage. The 1936/37 period was one in which rapid advances were being made in fighter design in many parts of the world and the steps taken by Curtiss designers led by Donovan R Berlin at this time were to lead to the introduction of one of the most important fighters available to the Allies in the early war years. This, the P-40, was in no way revolutionary; it was a straight-forward extrapolation of Hawk 75/P-36 design experience in which Curtiss sought to retain the excellent handling characteristics but enhance the performance of the basic product. The aircraft that resulted was not so far in advance of its contemporaries that it would have any distinct advantages in the battles to come; indeed, in almost every theatre in which it was deployed the P-40 proved to be inferior in performance to at least some of the types opposing it, especially at altitudes much above 10,000 ft (3 050 m). Yet it proved tractable and capable of absorbing much battle damage, was easy to produce in large quantities, and remained in large-scale production, in its later variants, until December 1944. The only relatively modern fighter available to the Army Air Force in quantity when the USA went to war, it was also supplied in large numbers to Allied air forces

including those of Britain, China, Canada, Australia, New Zealand, Brazil and the Soviet Union, and served in smaller numbers with several others.

Basically, the P-40 emerged as a P-36 with an in-line engine replacing the radial unit that powered all production variants of the Hawk 75. Two schemes were considered, in the 1936/37 time scale, for applying the Allison V-1720 12-cylinder Vee in-line liquid-cooled engine to this airframe. One, known initially as the Model 75-I, was built to Army Air Corps contract as the XP-37 in 1937 and was followed by 13 similar YP-37s for service test in 1939, but the use of turbo-superchargers to improve the altitude performance of an engine that was basically rated for sea level operation produced many problems and the venture was not successful.

The second attempt, Model 75-P, took advantage of Allison's work to rate the V-1710 for altitudes up to 15,000 ft (4 575 m) by use of a gear-driven supercharger that was likely to prove more reliable than the turbo-supercharger and in March 1938 Curtiss submitted a proposal to the Army Air Corps showing that a P-36 with this V-1710 could be expected to achieve 350 mph (563 km/h) at that altitude. As already explained in the account of the Bell P-39 (page 3) the Army Air Corps was at that time little interested in fighters with a good performance at altitude, since coastal defence and ground attack were considered to be the primary rôles for its fighters, but the Hawk 75-P proposal represented a sufficient advance over the P-36 to justify evaluation, and conversion of the 10th production P-36A airframe to have the new Allison engine was ordered, under the designation XP-40. Construction proceeded rapidly, and the XP-40 made its first flight on 14 October 1938, the pilot being E Elliott. Like the early P-36s, the prototype had one 0.50-in (12,7-mm) and one 0.30-in (7,62-mm) gun in the upper front fuselage, and the general structural details and configuration were similar to those of the Hawk 75. The carburetter air intake was on the upper cowling between the gun nozzles and an intake to the oil cooler was beneath the nose; the main radiator was in a ventral housing aft of the wing.

Powered by a V-1710-19 (C13) Allison engine, rated at 1,160 hp for take-off and capable of delivering 1,090 hp at 2,950 rpm at 10,000 ft (3 050 m), the XP-40 proved to be capable only of a disappointing 299 mph (481 km/h) but this was improved to 342 mph (550 km/h) when the radiator was moved forward to what would be its definitive position under the nose. In this form, the XP-40 participated in an Army Air Corps fighter competition at Wright Field on 25 January 1939, in which Curtiss also submitted the XP-37 and Hawk 75-R, the other contestants being the Lockheed XP-38, Bell XP-39 and Seversky AP-4. Notwithstanding the fact that both the Lockheed and Bell fighters would see large scale production in due course, the XP-40 was adjudged the clear winner, and plans for a large production contract were drawn up. Before this

(Above and below) Flight and ground views of the Curtiss XP-40 as first flown, with aft ventral radiator and rear-positioned carburettor air intake above the engine.

contract was confirmed, however, the Air Corps asked Curtiss to prove it could achieve the promised speed of 360 mph (579 km/h) at 15,000 ft (4575 m) and this was done, in March/April 1939, by introducing a number of relatively small drag-reducing modifications including enlarging the radiator fairing, removing mainwheel fairing plates, fitting individual exhaust stacks, repositioning the carburettor air intakes and using a redesigned tailwheel enclosure. The weight of the XP-40 at this stage was 5,417 lb (2 456 kg) empty, 6,260 lb (2 839 kg) with 100 US gal (378,5 l) of fuel and 6,870 lb (3 116 kg) with overload fuel of 158 US gal (598 l). Based on the use of an improved Allison V-1710-33 (C-15) engine rated at 1,040 hp for take-off, Curtiss now increased its guaranteed speed to 365 mph (587 km/h) and was rewarded, on 26 April 1939, with a contract for 524 P-40s at a cost of $12.8 m — the largest contract placed by the US War Department since 1918. In due course, Allison received an order for 969 engines.

Curtiss assigned a new model number, Hawk 81A, to the basic P-40 design, which in its initial production form for the US Army Air Corps had an armament of two 0.50-in (12,7-mm) M-2 Colt-Browning guns with 200 rpg and unprotected fuel tanks in the wing (102 US gal/385 l in two tanks) and the fuselage (58 US gal/218 l). No armour protection was provided and the windscreen did not make use of armoured glass — serious omissions for a fighter coming off the production lines in 1940. With a normal gross weight of 6,787 lb (3 078 kg), the P-40 demonstrated a max speed of 357 mph (574 km/h) at 15,000 ft (4 572 m), an initial rate of climb of 3,080 ft/min (15,65 m/sec) and a range of 950 mls (1 529 km) at 250 mph (402 km/h).

The first P-40 was flown on 4 April 1940 by Lloyd Childs, the company's chief test pilot, and service trials were undertaken with this aircraft and the next two, there being no prototypes as such. Army Air Corps acceptances began in May and by September a total of

(Above) The XP-40 after it had been modified to have the radiator intake ahead of the wing and (below) in its final guise with enlarged nose radiator and forward-positioned carburettor intake.

200 P-40s had been built. In that same month, the 8th Pursuit Group (33rd, 35th and 36th P Squadrons) began to convert to the type — which was unnamed by the Air Corps — at Langley Field, Virginia, and this became the first Group fully equipped with the new fighter, at the same time that the 20th PG at Marsh Field, California (55th, 77th and 79th Pursuit Squadrons) and the 31st PG at Selfridge Field, Mich (39th, 40th and 41st Pursuit Squadrons) began to convert to the type. By the spring of 1940, however, combat reports from Europe had made it clear to the Air Corps that its fighters were deficient in a number of respects by comparison with

An early production P-40 in flight in 1940. The P-40 was the first USAAC fighter to receive the olive drab finish, with grey undersides, at the factory. Tail stripes were deleted and fuselage stars added in March 1941.

contemporary British and German types, and the first steps were therefore taken to introduce a series of modifications designed to enhance the P-40's combat-worthiness. As Curtiss had succeeded in selling an export version of the aircraft to France and Britain, production of which carried a high priority following President Roosevelt's decision of 25 March 1940 to allow friendly nations to purchase the latest types of American combat aircraft, the Air Corps could conveniently delay production of the balance of its original P-40 order, and deliveries were not resumed until early in 1941, when the improved P-40B became available.

The new features of this model included a hardened windscreen, a small armour plate installed in front of the pilot plus a larger backplate and self-sealing fuel tanks. The firepower was virtually doubled by installing a 0.30-in (7,62-mm) Colt-Browning in each wing and increasing the ammunition for the nose-mounted weapons to 380 rpg. The engine was unchanged, and at a gross weight of 6,835 lb (3 100 kg), the P-40B achieved a speed of 352 mph (566 km/h) at 15,000 ft (4 572 m). The normal loaded weight had increased, however, to 7,325 lb (3 322 kg) and with the consequent increase in wing loading and decrease in power loading there was an inevitable deterioration in manoeuvrability.

With the original P-40s now regarded as little better than trainers, the P-40Bs were the first of the new Curtiss fighters to be deployed overseas, and no time was lost in getting these aircraft to US outstations in Hawaii and the Philippines. By the end of April squadrons of the 15th and 18th Pursuit Groups, based at Wheeler Field, Hawaii, had received 55 P-40Bs, transported aboard US Navy aircraft carriers and flown off upon arrival, and another 31 had arrived, crated, in the Philippines to be used by the 20th Pursuit Squadron

of the 24th PG at Clark Field. Production of the P-40B totalled 131, when a switch was made to the P-40C, which embodied a new fuel system with self-sealing tanks having a total capacity of 134 US gal (507 l) plus provision for a 52 US gal (197 l) drop tank under the fuselage. Radio equipment was improved, an SCR-247N set replacing the SCR-283, and wing armament was doubled, to four 0.30-in (7,62-mm) Brownings and 490 rpg. The gross weight went up again, to 8,058 lb (3,658 kg).

The first P-40C flew on 10 April 1941 and production of 324 completed the original Air Corps contract for 524 aircraft. Deliveries began before the end of April, the Curtiss production effort by this time being in high gear with 30 production test pilots on hand and assembled aircraft frequently being flown out of the car park adjacent to the Kenmore Plant to nearby Buffalo Municipal Airport to save road haulage time — the take-off strip being 1,100 ft (336 m) long and a few inches wider than the P-40's wing.

Deliveries of P-40Cs from April 1941 onwards allowed additional overseas units to equip with the type — the 35th Squadron of the 36th PG going to Puerto Rico in April and the 16th PG (24th, 29th and 43rd Pursuit Squadrons) taking a mixture of 70 P-40Bs and P-40Cs to Panama. In August, the original P-40 unit, the 8th PG, detached its 33rd Squadron to Iceland with 30 P-40Cs. In Hawaii, 12 P-40Cs had arrived to augment 87 P-40Bs by the time of the Japanese attack on 7 December, and were attached to the 44th Pursuit Squadron, 18th PG at Bellows. The P-40Bs were mostly at Wheeler Field, where they equipped the 45th and 47th Pursuit Squadrons of the 15th PG — the latter unit having eight of its aircraft detached to Haleiwa for gunnery training — and the 6th, 19th, 73rd and 78th Pursuit Squadrons of the 18th PG. At all bases, on the morning of 7 December, the P-40s were lined up, as was customary, with empty fuel tanks and guns unloaded, and at least 62 P-40Bs were destroyed on the ground at Wheeler Field in the first Japanese attack. Three P-40Cs got airborne from Bellows, which had been alerted by a single Japanese attacker, but two were shot down by a second strike of six Zero fighters that arrived at the same time and seven of the nine P-40Cs remaining on the ground were destroyed. Four P-40Bs of the 47th Pursuit Squadron took off from Haleiwa and landed at Wheeler Field without making contact with the enemy, but in two subsequent sorties from Wheeler during the day,

(Above left) This P-40 was assigned to Pratt & Whitney to serve as a test-bed for the R-1830 Twin Wasp radial. (Below left) A P-40B, with one gun in each wing, in service with the 55th Squadron, 35th Pursuit Group and (right) a P-40C of the 77th Squadron, 20th Pursuit Group.

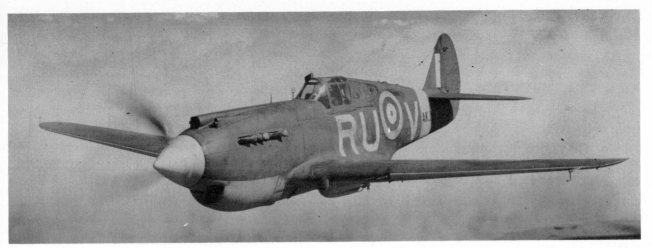

Curtiss Hawk 81A-1s ordered by France were supplied to the RAF as Tomahawk Is and were followed by similar Tomahawk IIs (above and below left), used to equip army co-operation squadrons in the UK and fighter squadrons in the Western Desert.

Wasp radial, housed in a specially-designed close-cowling, and another was a P-40 fitted, during July 1940, with a four-gun wing of the type adopted by Britain on its Hawk 81-A2s. This variant was eventually designated P-40G and 44 more were later produced for the USAAF by using spare or partially damaged airframes for which new wings were built. The original P-40G was included in an initial batch of 21 P-40s supplied to the Soviet Union in 1940, but the later P-40Gs served, from 1942, with the Air Base Groups at Pope Field, Marsh Field and Hamilton Field. With the passage of the Lend-Lease Act in May 1941, plans were made to transfer 10 P-40Bs to Yugoslavia, but this did not occur and after being provisionally re-assigned to the RAF, they were retained by the USAAC. Later, in March 1942, one P-40 was fitted with cameras for the fighter-reconnaissance rôle and designated P-40A.

Britain's Tomahawks

On 9 October 1939, the French Purchasing Commission in the USA placed an order with Curtiss-Wright for 230 Hawk 81A-1s on behalf of *l'Armée de l'Air*, which was already receiving Hawk 75As. Approval for the export of these aircraft was withheld by the US government until March 1940, however, by which time production was well in hand. By 31 May, 57 of these Hawk 81A-1s had been crated ready for despatch to France although no acceptance flights had been made by French pilots. Intended to be assembled at Bourges, like the Hawk 75As, the Hawk 81As were not in fact delivered to France at all, the entire contract being taken over by the British Purchasing Commission upon the collapse of France.

For France, the Hawk 81A-1s were basically similar to the USAAC's P-40 but had the Radio-Industrie 537 radio in place of the SCR-283, a modified seat to accommodate the Lemercier back-parachute, French instrumentation and throttle operation and provision for a Baille-Lemaire gunsight and Munerelle oxygen sysem (to be installed after delivery). The armament was

these P-40B pilots claimed the destruction of five Japanese aircraft. By the end of the day, two P-40Cs and 25 P-40Bs remained airworthy in Hawaii.

Meanwhile, in the Philippines, the 24th Pursuit Group faired no better. Its 18 operational P-40Bs of the 20th Pursuit Squadron had been supplemented by P-40Es (see Hawk 87, page 54) in service with the 17th, 21st and 3rd Pursuit Squadrons, and during the day a total of 26 of the Curtiss fighters was lost — almost entirely on the ground at Clark Field — although the first aerial victory of the war in the Philippine area went to a P-40B of the 20th PS. The P-40Es, as related later, achieved some success and the CO of the 17th Pursuit Squadron, Lt Col Boyd D Wagner, became the first US "ace" of the war in the process, but the 24th PG as a whole was wiped out within a few weeks, some of its pilots being evacuated to Australia and others fighting on against overwhelming odds in the Philippines until May 1942.

The pressing need for operational fighters during 1941/42 meant that almost all the original production batch of P-40s, P-40Bs and P-40Cs went into service. One exception was the example supplied to Pratt & Whitney to serve as a test-bed for the 1,200 hp Twin

to comprise four 7,5-mm FN-Browning Mle 38 machine guns in the wings supplementing the two 0.50-in (12,7-mm) M-2 Colt-Brownings in the upper front fuselage. In this guise, those aircraft already built for France and those in an advanced stage of manufacture, totalling 140, were shipped to the UK, where they were given the name Tomahawk I by the RAF. Four 0.303-in (7,7-mm) Browning guns were fitted in the empty wing bays (the fuselage guns being already installed), the minimum of British equipment and radio was installed and the throttles were modified, but lacking armour protection and self-sealing fuel tanks, these aircraft were judged unsuitable for use as interceptors in a rôle that might involve air-to-air combat. With the possibility of an imminent German invasion of the British Isles, however, the Tomahawks could not be completely disregarded, and it was decided that they would be used in the Army Co-operation rôle for low-altitude tactical reconnaissance.

Modifications were ordered for the balance of 90 French-contract aircraft, comprising the use of armour-glass windscreen, some armour protection for the pilot and self-sealing fuel tanks, and, being fully-armed in the USA before delivery, these aircraft had 0.30-in (7,62-mm) Colt-Browning machine guns in the wings. Designated Hawk 81A-2 by Curtiss, these 90 fighters plus the first 20 of a total of 950 ordered on direct British contract were known as Tomahawk IIAs to the RAF. The balance of 930 on the British order were Tomahawk IIBs, which reverted to having 0.303-in (7,7-mm) wing guns and had British rather than US radio and oxygen equipment. Nearly half of this total had been delivered by the end of 1940, the remainder following rapidly in 1941. The last 300 Tomahawk IIBs (the first of which flew on 23 April 1941) were known as Hawk 81A-3s to Curtiss, having the revised fuel system and increased ammunition capacity of the P-40C, with provision for a 43 Imp-gal (197-l) belly drop tank. In addition to the total of 1,180 Tomahawks acquired on the ex-French and British contracts, the RAF took on

charge three other early model P-40s of unknown origin (serial numbers AX900, BK852 and BK853).

Pending the arrival of the somewhat more battle-worthy Tomahawk IIs, the Tomahawk Is were issued to Nos 2, 26, 171, 231, 239, 268 and 613 Squadrons RAF and Nos 400 and 403 Squadrons, RCAF, all based in the UK, for use on conversion training and preliminary operations. The Tomahawk IIAs and IIBs supplanted the Mk Is, serving primarily with Nos 2, 26, 231, 239 and 241 Squadrons RAF, and the RCAF Nos 400 and 414. Between March and October 1941, a total of 294 Tomahawks was assigned to the Middle East, including 89 shipped direct from the USA and the others despatched from the UK, for assembly at Takoradi on the Gold Coast.

No 250 Squadron became the first to convert to the Curtiss fighter in the Middle East, in May 1941, followed by the RAAF's No 3 Squadron and the SAAF's No 2 Squadron. By November, these units had been joined in the Western desert by No 112 RAF and No 4 SAAF, also on Tomahawk IIBs; No 73 Squadron RAF had flown the type briefly but re-equipped with Hurricanes in that month, but in February and March 1942, Nos 260 Squadron RAF and Nos 5 and 40 Squadrons, SAAF, also began operating Tomahawks in North Africa. Modest "tropicalization" of the Tomahawks comprised the fitting of dust filters on the carburettor air intakes and some aircraft had 0.303-in (7,7-mm) machine guns fitted in place of the larger calibre fuselage guns, to simplify ammunition supply.

By the spring of 1941, with the Battle of Britain over, the immediate threat of a German invasion receding and supplies of superior fighters building up, the RAF was able to make some of its Tomahawks available to other users. The first such arrangement provided for the sale of 100 Hawk 81A-2s, originally intended as Tomahawk IIBs, to the Chinese National Government for use by the American Volunteer Group (AVG, better known as the "Flying Tigers") then being formed, with the co-operation of the US government, by General

General Claire Chennault's famous Flying Tigers, a group of American volunteers flying in the China/Burma/India theatre in 1940/41, initially flew Hawk 81A-2s released by Britain and adopted the shark's teeth marking originally used on No 112 Squadron, RAF, Tomahawks in the Western Desert.

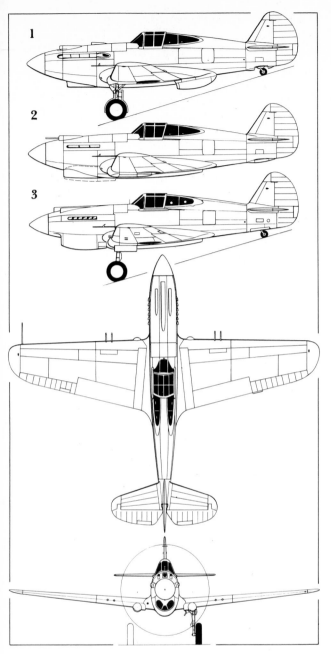

The line drawings above depict (1), the original XP-40, (2), the XP-40 as first and (dotted line) later modified and (3), a three-view of the Curtiss P-40C.

Claire L Chennault. The AVG was formed at an RAF base at Toungoo, Burma, with the primary objective of defending the central portion of the Burma Road between Chungking and Lashio, this being the principal supply route into China, and its 100 Hawk 81A-2s — which were always referred to simply as P-40s by the AVG itself — arrived by sea in Rangoon in June 1941. They were erected and test flown at Rangoon and then flown up to Toungoo by AVG pilots — who for the most part were recruited from USAAF pursuit and bombing squadrons — in the period from 3 August to 28 November 1941.

Immediately following the attack on Pearl Harbor, Chennault moved the AVG to an unfinished airstrip at Kunming at the eastern end of the Burma Road. The Group was divided into three 18-aircraft squadrons (the 1st, 2nd and 3rd) but training accidents and lack of spares often reduced the numbers of aircraft available to below this level. The 3rd Squadron was detailed to Mingaledon, Rangoon, to reinforce No 67 Squadron, RAF, with its outdated Buffaloes, and the 1st and 2nd Squadrons flew the AVG's first combat mission on 20 December from Kunming, intercepting 10 unescorted Ki-21 bombers and destroying six. The 3rd Squadron saw action three days later over Rangoon, claiming 10 Japanese aircraft destroyed for the loss of three P-40s and two pilots, and the Group then fought at a high level of activity for six months, principally over Burma, in which time it claimed a total of 286 Japanese aircraft destroyed. The original Hawk 81A-2s were later supplemented by 30 P-40Es and the AVG was absorbed into the USAAF on 5 July 1942 as the 23rd Pursuit Group, within China Air Task Force (commanded by Chennault). This unit, starting life with 27 of the original Hawks plus 24 P-40Es, continued to operate in the same area, and with the same spirit, as the AVG, but newer models of the P-40 soon began to reach the area, in which they fought with distinction until the end of the War.

During 1941, small numbers of RAF Tomahawks in the Middle East were made available to the Royal Egyptian Air Force and the Turkish Air Force. Also in 1941, 146 Tomahawks were shipped to the Soviet Union from the UK, and the last 49 examples built on British contract were also shipped to that destination direct from the USA. In Russia, they joined 20 P-40s and the original P-40G that had been despatched by the US government between July and October 1940, being used by the V-VS (*Voenno-vozdushniye Sily*) for the defence of strategic targets. One of the first Tomahawk-equipped units in the V-VS was the 125IAP (125th Fighter Regiment) attached to the Eastern Sector of the Moscow PVO, but lack of spares and other factors kept utilisation of the early P-40s by the V-VS at a low level.

Curtiss P-40C Specification
Power Plant: One Allison V-1710-33 12-cylinder Vee liquid-cooled engine rated at 1,040 hp for take-off and 1,090 hp at 13,200 ft (4 026 m). Fuel capacity, 160 US gal (606 l) in wing and fuselage tanks.
Performance: Max speed (at 7,327 lb/3 323 kg), 345 mph (555 km/h) at 15,000 ft (4 572 m); max continuous cruise, 270 mph (434 km/h); initial rate of climb, 2,690 ft/min (13,66 m/sec); service ceiling, 29,500 ft (8 990 m); range, 800 mls (1 287 km).
Weights: Empty equipped, 5,812 lb (2 636 kg); normal loaded, 7,549 lb (3 424 kg); max, 8,058 lb (3 655 kg).
Dimensions: Span, 37 ft 3½ in (11,37 m); length, 31 ft 8½ in (9,66 m); height, 10 ft 7 in (3,22 m); wing area, 236 sq ft (21,92 m²).
Armament: Two 0.50-in (12,7-mm) Colt-Browning machine guns in upper front fuselage with 380 rpg and four 0.30-in (7,62-mm) Colt-Browning machine guns in wings, with 490 rpg.

The Hawk 87 was the final production form of the long series of Curtiss Hawk fighters, remaining in service in many combat areas until the end of the war. The initial Hawk 87 model for the US Army was the P-40D, illustrated above.

Curtiss Hawk 87 (P-40 Warhawk and Kittyhawk)

With production of the Hawk 81 variants in full swing for the USAAC and the RAF in 1940, Curtiss and Allison turned their attention to improving the basic fighter by intoroducing an engine of increased performance. This engine, the Allison V-1710-39 (F3R), offered a take-off rating of 1,150 hp, which could be maintained as a military rating at 11,700 ft (3 566 m); it also had a 5-min war emergency rating of 1,470 hp, a feature lacking in the Tomahawk and P-40. With an external spur airscrew reduction gear supplanting the internal spur of the earlier V-1710-33, this new engine was shorter and had a raised thrust line. Consequently, its installation in the P-40 airframe called for some modification of the forward contours; the radiator had to be enlarged and was positioned farther forward, and the higher thrust line allowed the undercarriage to be a little shorter, while the cross section of the fuselage was very slightly reduced. The fuselage guns had to be omitted because of the revised nose contours, and the wing armament was therefore increased to four 0.5-in (12,7-mm) guns, with new hydraulic chargers.

With few changes in the basic structure and systems, compared with the Hawk 81, the Hawk 87 could be phased into production with relative ease, and the British Purchasing Commission was quick to take advantage of the extra potential offered by the uprated engine, placing an order in May 1940 for 560 Hawk 87s, to be known to the RAF as Kittyhawks. The USAAC soon followed suit, deciding in June to order a version of the Hawk 87 as the P-40D in place of the similarly-powered P-46 (see page 68), the production of which could not proceed so rapidly. The first flight of the new Curtiss type followed on 22 May 1941, the aircraft in question being the first of the British contract.

During July 1941, the USAAF (as the Army Air Corps became on 20 June) took delivery of 22 P-40Ds (Hawk 87A-1s) but four months previously the specification had been changed to increase the wing armament from four to six guns. In this guise, the Air Force version was designated P-40E, and the name Warhawk was adopted for this and subsequent versions; the RAF, on the other hand, made no distinction between its first 20 Kittyhawks with four guns and the balance of 540 with six guns, all being Mk I aircraft (Hawk 87A-2). With 175 lb (80 kg) of armour plate fitted, the P-40Es could also carry a 500-lb (227,5-kg) bomb beneath the fuselage in lieu of the 52 US gal (197-l) drop tank. The combat weight increased to 8,400 lb (3816 kg) with a maximum overlaod weight of 9,200 lb (4177 kg) with full internal tanks and the external bomb. Radio equipment comprised either the SCR-283 or SCR-274N set and later production P-40Es had provision for two 100-lb (45-kg) or six 20-lb (9,1-kg) bombs to be carried under the wings.

The USAAF acquired a total of 820 P-40Es, with deliveries starting on 29 August 1941; consequently, initial deployment of the new Warhawks was still under way when the USA went to war. By comparison with the Hawk 81A series, the Hawk 87A was faster at all altitudes, although by only a relatively small margin; it offered an improved weight of fire, was more combat-worthy and could carry bombs (a feature available on the Hawk 81s only by improvisation in the field), but the rate of climb was reduced and take-off performance suffered as a result of the increased weight. Manoeuvrability — never the strongest feature of the Hawk 81A — was markedly inferior, and the redistributed loading of the later model rendered it much more sensitive on the controls, demanding close concentration on the part of the pilot during low-level runs and causing considerable trim changes during a dive. Stick forces grew very heavy in the dive, considerable force being necessary to pull out at speeds approaching 400 mph (644 km/h) and there was a strong tendency to skid. The Hawk 87A was prone to swing on take-off — to overcome which a small dorsal fin extension was designed and applied to some aircraft as a field modification; pending the introduction of later variants with more extensive redesign of the rear fuselage — and directional stability at low speeds was poor. The introduction of this new model therefore called for careful training and indoctrination of the pilots, but in the exigencies of the first few months of American involvement in combat, this was a luxury that could not be afforded, and the service debut of the P-40E was accordingly inauspicious.

When hostilities began in the Pacific, a total of 74 P-40Es had been delivered to Army Air Force units in the Philippines, for use by the 24th Pursuit Group (3rd, 17th, 20th, 21st and 34th Pursuit Squadrons); starting in September, the 3rd PS had re-equipped on the Warhawk at Iba Field and the 17th PS at Nichols Field, while during November the 21st PS began to convert, also at Nichols Field. Many of these P-40Es, together with the P-40Bs still equipping the 20th PS, and other types, were destroyed on the ground in the initial Japanese attacks, and by the end of December 1941, only 38 P-40Es (plus eight P-40Bs) remained serviceable. The 24th PG was in constant action during the next few days, as Japanese troops began the invasion of the Philippine Islands, and in this period the CO of the 17th PS, Lt Boyd D "Buzz" Wagner, became the first American "ace" of World War II with the destruction of two Mitsubishi Ki-27 ("Nate") fighters on 12 December and four more the next day. Cut off from supplies, however, the US forces in the Philippines were fighting against impossible odds and the force of P-40s had been

reduced to 18 by 26 December, when the 17th, 21st and 34th PS were merged into a single unit. The remnants of this unit eventually concentrated upon Bataan Field with seven P-40Es and two P-40Bs, forming the Bataan Field Flying Detachment, its 20 pilots being drawn from all the squadrons of the 24th PG. From mid-January to early April 1942, a steadily dwindling number of P-40s maintained a constant effort of strafing, bombing and reconnaissance over the Japanese invaders, scoring at least 12 aerial victories in the process; one surviving Warhawk flew out of Bataan on the day its defenders surrendered, to join four other

(Above) A ground view of the P-40D and (below) a P-40E, with wing armament increased from four to six machine guns, serving with the 77th Squadron, 20th Pursuit Group.

(Below) Although P-40Es had not reached Hawaii by the time of the Japanese attack at the end of 1941, enough were in service in the US to participate in the annual War Games earlier in the year; these are aircraft of the 77th Squadron, 20th Pursuit Group, specially marked for the purpose.

Serving in Egypt in 1943, this Merlin-engined P-40L wears desert camouflage and the RAF tail stripes that were applied to all Allied aircraft in the area. A P-40L-10, this Warhawk also displays the lengthened rear fuselage, compared with the short-fuselage Merlin-engined P-40F (below).

P-40Es that were still flying from airstrips in northern Mindanao, these all being destroyed by US personnel when the final surrender in the Philippines was ordered on 6 May 1942.

Meanwhile, urgent efforts had been made to reform the 24th Pursuit Group in Australia, where some pilots of the 17th PS had arrived upon being evacuated from the Philippines, and 198 P-40Es were allocated to Australia, for eventual use in Java. On 14 January 1940, 17 P-40Es of the 17th PS (Provisional) left for Java and another 55 were despatched soon after in the hands of the 3rd, 20th and 33rd PS (Provisional), but a combination of pilot inexperience, navigational errors and inclement weather resulted in most of these being lost *en route*, and only 38 P-40Es ever achieved combat status in Java, these being quickly overwhelmed. The squadrons of the 24th Pursuit Group were not again reformed, although the Group did remain on the active list until 1946. Some 30 P-40Es originally destined for Java were diverted while at sea, to Takoradi, on the Gold Coast, where they arrived in March 1942 and were eventually collected by pilots of the American Volunteer Group in China, these being ferried the 6,000 mls (9 650 km) to Kunming to supplement that unit's surviving Hawk 81A-2s.

After the AVG had been absorbed by the USAAF to become the 23rd Fighter Group (74th, 75th and 76th FS) in July 1942, it continued operations with a mix of P-40Es and Hawk 81A-2s, being reinforced later in the year by the 16th FS, detached from the 51st FG in India and flying P-40Es. Always fighting in conditions of extreme difficulty, with few supplies and no luxuries to make the life of the personnel more bearable, these squadrons fought in the China theatre to the end of the war, with P-40Ks eventually supplementing the P-40Es.

By the spring of 1942, too, P-40Es were reaching Alaska, to be used by the 11th and 18th Pursuit Squadrons attached to the 28th Composite Group. These two squadrons were engaged in combat in June when Japanese forces attacked Dutch Harbor; flying from poorly equipped airstrips at Cold By and Umnak, they had little success in intercepting the bombing formations, but destroyed two floatplanes launched by Japanese cruisers on reconnaissance missions.

While the RAF had been receiving its initial batch of Kittyhawk Is in parallel with USAAF's P-40Es, the passage of the Lend-Lease Act earlier in 1941 had made it possible for additional quantities of the Curtiss fighter to be put in hand for Britain. Under the usual Lend-Lease arrangements, contracts were placed by the USAAF, and all aircraft so produced therefore were assigned USAAF designations and serial numbers for contractural purposes. The first such orders for Hawk 87s comprised two batches of P-40E-1s (Hawk 87A-4) totalling 1,500 aircraft, all of which were assigned to Britain as Kittyhawk IAs (use of an 'A' suffix became standard practice for Lend-Lease equivalents of aircraft already purchased by Britain; types supplied exclusively under Lend-Lease were not so distinguished). Deliveries began in September 1941 and continued to June 1942, almost all of these aircraft being shipped direct to Africa for use in the Western Desert (as described later) or supplied, through British arrangements, to the RAAF, RCAF or RNZAF.

Seeking a means of improving the altitude performance of the P-40, Curtiss had proposed the installation of a Rolls-Royce Merlin 28, featuring a single-stage two-speed supercharger, and the Army Air Corps had agreed, early in 1941, to allow such an installation to proceed in the second production P-40D airframe. Redesignated XP-40F, this made its first flight on 30 June 1941 and on the basis of successful flight testing, production contracts were placed for an eventual total of 1,311 P-40Fs. In its production form, the P-40F was powered by a Packard-built V-1650-1 Merlin, rated at 1,300 hp for take-off and giving 1,240 hp at 11,500 ft (3 505 m) and 1,120 hp at 18,500 ft (5 638 m). Armament was unchanged from the P-40E, comprising the six wing guns plus provision for bombs or fuel tanks, but careful redesign of the fuel tanks in the wings and fuselage increased the internal capacity by 8 US gal (30 l) and provision was made for larger belly drop tanks to be carried — of 75, 150 or 170 US gal (284, 568 or 643 l) capacity. Removal of the carburettor air intake from the top of the cowling, to be incorporated in the radiator scoop, made the Merlin engine installation readily distinguishable from the Allison variants.

The third production P-40F was used for experiments with the radiator position, a deep aft-positioned ventral radiator bath being fitted for comparative purposes with the standard configuration, but this showed no performance advantages. After production of 699 P-40F-1s, Curtiss introduced a lengthened rear fuselage, with a 19-in (48-cm) section inserted under the tailplane, to improve directional stability at low speeds, the vertical tail surfaces being moved farther aft in relation to the horizontal surfaces. This configuration applied to the P-40F-5 to P-40F-20 production batches; the P-40F-10 introduced electric cowl flap actuation in place of manual, the -15 batch were winterized for Alaskan service and the -20s had demand- instead of constant-flow oxygen system. Of the total P-40F production, 330 were assigned to Britain under Lend-Lease, being designated Kittyhawk II by the RAF.

Deliveries of the P-40F began in January 1942, and four months later the USAAF also began to receive another new Warhawk version, the P-40K. This was essentially a P-40E fitted with the more powerful Allison V-1710-73 (F4R) engine, with a 1,325 hp take-off rating and delivering 1,150 hp in military rating at 11,800 ft (3 600 m). The fuel capacity was the same as that for the P-40F and performance was little changed from that of the P-40E. An initial order for 600 P-40K-1s was placed through Lend-Lease channels with the intention that these aircraft should be supplied to China, but only a few reached this destination, the majority going into USAAF service in the China/Burma/India theatre or being supplied to the Soviet Union. Additional orders produced 200 P-40K-2s, which like the K-1s had the original short fuselage and a small dorsal fin, and then 500 K-10 and K-15 models with the lengthened fuselage, delivery being completed by the end of 1942. The RAF used the designation Kittyhawk III for 21 P-40Ks received through Lend-

Lease, together with its P-40Ms described below.

The designation P-40H had been discarded and the P-40J was a projected version with an Allison engine and a turbo-supercharger, studied in parallel with the P-40F. One P-40K was redesignated XP-40K when used for a drag reduction exercise, in which the nose radiator scoop was removed and a revised cooling system was fitted, with radiators mounted in a swollen wing centre section. The next production versions, therefore, built almost entirely for supply to America's Allies, were the P-40L and P-40M. The P-40L was Merlin-engined, like the P-40F, the 50 short-fuselage P-40L-1s differing from the latter only in minor details. The P-40L was primarily intended, however, to be a light-weight version, performance being improved by removing two of the wing guns and the 37 US gal (140 l) forward wing fuel tank, and reducing the ammunition for the remaining four guns from 281 to 201 rpg. Thus stripped, the P-40L acquired the appellation "Gypsy Rose Lee" after the famous strip-tease dancer of the period, and production totalled 650 in versions P-40L-5 to L-20, all with the long fuselage; deliveries were made in the first four months of 1943. In the following year, a shortage of Merlin spares led to the modification of about 300 P-40F and P-40L Warhawks to have Allison V-1710-81 engines, in which guise they were designated P-40R-1 and P-40R-2 respectively.

Produced in parallel with the P-40L, the P-40M was intended specifically for use by Commonwealth Air Forces, and introduced the V-1710-81 engine, which was rated at 1,200 hp for take-off and delivered 1,125 hp at 17,300 ft (5 273 m). Apart from this engine change,

Curtiss made a number of experiments directed at improving the engine cooling system and/or reducing the aerodynamic drag of the P-40. Examples were (above) the YP-40F with aft radiator and (below) the YP-40K with wing root air intakes replacing the nose air scoop.

(Above) Carrying small bombs on the fuselage pylons, three P-40Fs of the 324th Fighter Group fly over Tunisia in the closing days of the war in Africa. (Below left) A P-40K-1 in desert colours, showing drop tank and small dorsal fin extension.

the P-40M was virtually identical with the P-40K, but its performance was usefully improved, the speed being 360 mph (579 km/h) at 20,000 ft (6 100 m) and 353 mph (568 km/h) at 25,000 ft (7 620 m). The climbing performance was also better, especially at medium altitudes — time to 15,000 ft (4 570 m) was reduced by 1 min and to 25,000 ft (7 620 m) by 4 min. Production of the P-40M totalled 600 and all but five of these were assigned to the RAF as Kittyhawk IIIs, although not all were in fact delivered.

Following upon deliveries of the P-40Ms, completed in February 1943, came the first of the P-40Ns, which proved to be the most-produced of all Warhawk versions, despite the fact that the type was now rapidly becoming outmoded and its inadequate performance was becoming a cause for widespread concern. The primary reason for the continuation of Warhawk production at this time was the considerable momentum that the programme had achieved coupled with the high demand for Lend-Lease supplies, particularly for the Soviet Union. The USAAF naturally had first call on the output of more advanced types from other factories, and any attempt to switch the Curtiss factories to the production of a different type, or even a major modification of the P-40, would have caused serious delays in the delivery of aircraft to the Allies. The P-40N was an attempted compromise to obtain improved performance from the basic Warhawk without interrupting volume production.

First ordered early in 1943, the P-40N introduced a new light-weight structure and was subjected to a rigid component survey placing emphasis on weight saving. Aluminium oil coolers and radiators were incorporated, as well as lighter wheels and, as in the P-40L-5, the forward wing tank and two wing guns were omitted, with the ammunition capacity for the

A Curtiss P-40N, the final Warhawk production version; among the features of note are the lengthened rear fuselage, the DF loop and the modified rear cockpit.

(Right) The drawings show: (1), the P-40D and E; (2), long-fuselage P-40F and L side, plan and head-on views; (3), original P-40F and L short fuselage; (4), P-40K, with long-fuselage dotted; (5), P-40M; (6), P-40N showing revised cockpit and)7), two-seat TP-40N.

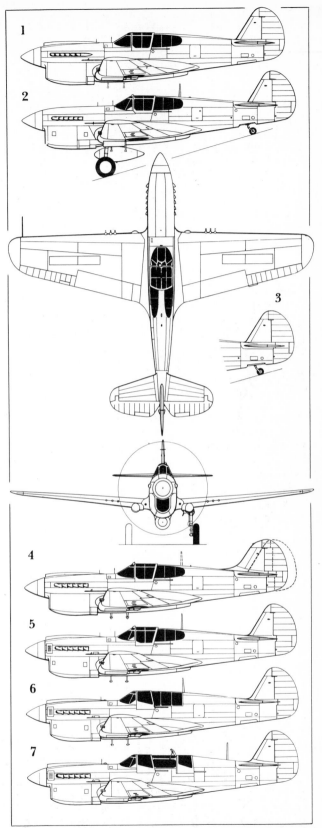

remaining guns reduced. With the same V-1710-81 engine as the P-40M, the P-40N had an empty weight of 6,400 lb (2 903 kg), the combat weight being 7,725 lb (3 504 kg) compared with 8,400 lb (3 814 kg), and the speed being 378 mph (608 km/h) at 10,500 ft (3 200 m) — the fastest attained by any Warhawk model.

Orders for the P-40N were placed on an unprecedented scale, eventually totalling 6,000 although 785 of these were subsequently cancelled. After 400 P-40N-1s had been built, however, the full six-gun armament was restored in the P-40N-5, and this sub-variant also introduced other major changes of which the most obvious was a modified cockpit canopy with a frameless sliding hood and a deeper, rectangular aft section to improve the view rearwards. Provision was made, on the -5, for two 225-US gal (841-l) ferry tanks or two 500-lb (227-kg) bombs to be carried under the wings, in addition to the fuselage bomb as on earlier models. Production of 1,577 P-40N-5, -10 and -15 Warhawks was completed by September 1943, and a switch was then made to the V-1710-99 engine in the P-40N-20, this having the same output as the -81 engine but provision for a manifold presure modifier. Improved non-metallic self-sealing fuel tanks, new radio and oxygen equipment and flame-damping exhausts were progressively introduced and 3,022 examples of the P-40N-20, -25, -30 and -35 were built. Finally came 216 P-40N-40s which had the V-1710-115 engine with automatic boost and propeller controls. The last production Warhawk, P-40N-40, serial 44-47964, left the Curtiss Buffalo plant on 30 November 1944; of the total of 5,215 P-40Ns built, 536 were allocated to Britain and designated Kittyhawk IV.

Thirty P-40N-5s were modified before delivery by Curtiss to two-seat trainers, an instructor's cockpit being located in the fuselage behind the regular cockpit and provided with a periscope to improve forward view. These were designated TP-40N-6, and several similar conversions of P-40Ns were undertaken in the field by USAAF maintenance units. The first two-seat Warhawks had, in fact, been a pair of P-40Es, similarly modified and designated P-40ES.

One final effort had also been made to improve the Warhawk's performance, when a P-40K airframe was fitted with an Allison V-1710-121 engine rated at 1,425 hp for take-off and 1,100 hp at 25,000 ft (7 620 m). This was cooled by means of semi-flush, low-drag radiators embodied in the wing centre section. With a four-bladed propeller, this prototype was redesignated XP-40Q; a second XP-40Q, similarly modified from a P-40K, had the same engine installation but a forward radiator and an all-round vision "bubble" canopy, and a third XP-40Q was a modified P-40N-20 with features similar to the second XP-40Q but clipped wings with a span of 35 ft 3 in (10,75 m). With water injection, this XP-40Q achieved 422 mph (679 km/h) at 20,500 ft (6 250 m) during trials in 1944, climbing to 20,000 ft (6 100 m) in 4.8 min.

Of the grand total of 13,738 Hawk 81A and 87A

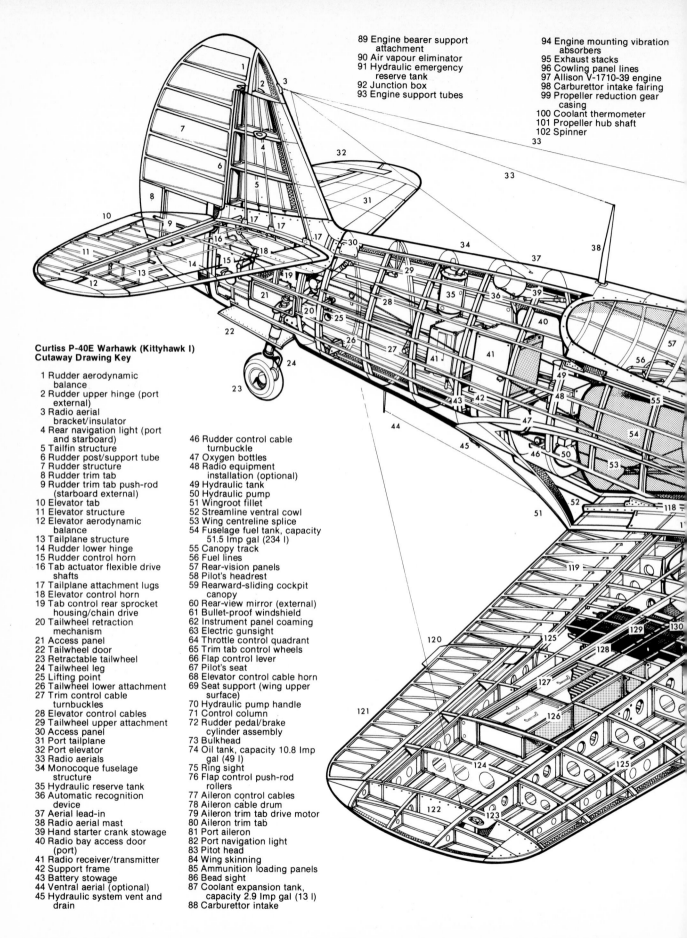

89 Engine bearer support attachment
90 Air vapour eliminator
91 Hydraulic emergency reserve tank
92 Junction box
93 Engine support tubes

94 Engine mounting vibration absorbers
95 Exhaust stacks
96 Cowling panel lines
97 Allison V-1710-39 engine
98 Carburettor intake fairing
99 Propeller reduction gear casing
100 Coolant thermometer
101 Propeller hub shaft
102 Spinner

Curtiss P-40E Warhawk (Kittyhawk I) Cutaway Drawing Key

1 Rudder aerodynamic balance
2 Rudder upper hinge (port external)
3 Radio aerial bracket/insulator
4 Rear navigation light (port and starboard)
5 Tailfin structure
6 Rudder post/support tube
7 Rudder structure
8 Rudder trim tab
9 Rudder trim tab push-rod (starboard external)
10 Elevator tab
11 Elevator structure
12 Elevator aerodynamic balance
13 Tailplane structure
14 Rudder lower hinge
15 Rudder control horn
16 Tab actuator flexible drive shafts
17 Tailplane attachment lugs
18 Elevator control horn
19 Tab control rear sprocket housing/chain drive
20 Tailwheel retraction mechanism
21 Access panel
22 Tailwheel door
23 Retractable tailwheel
24 Tailwheel leg
25 Lifting point
26 Tailwheel lower attachment
27 Trim control cable turnbuckles
28 Elevator control cables
29 Tailwheel upper attachment
30 Access panel
31 Port tailplane
32 Port elevator
33 Radio aerials
34 Monocoque fuselage structure
35 Hydraulic reserve tank
36 Automatic recognition device
37 Aerial lead-in
38 Radio aerial mast
39 Hand starter crank stowage
40 Radio bay access door (port)
41 Radio receiver/transmitter
42 Support frame
43 Battery stowage
44 Ventral aerial (optional)
45 Hydraulic system vent and drain

46 Rudder control cable turnbuckle
47 Oxygen bottles
48 Radio equipment installation (optional)
49 Hydraulic tank
50 Hydraulic pump
51 Wingroot fillet
52 Streamline ventral cowl
53 Wing centreline splice
54 Fuselage fuel tank, capacity 51.5 Imp gal (234 l)
55 Canopy track
56 Fuel lines
57 Rear-vision panels
58 Pilot's headrest
59 Rearward-sliding cockpit canopy
60 Rear-view mirror (external)
61 Bullet-proof windshield
62 Instrument panel coaming
63 Electric gunsight
64 Throttle control quadrant
65 Trim tab control wheels
66 Flap control lever
67 Pilot's seat
68 Elevator control cable horn
69 Seat support (wing upper surface)
70 Hydraulic pump handle
71 Control column
72 Rudder pedal/brake cylinder assembly
73 Bulkhead
74 Oil tank, capacity 10.8 Imp gal (49 l)
75 Ring sight
76 Flap control push-rod rollers
77 Aileron control cables
78 Aileron cable drum
79 Aileron trim tab drive motor
80 Aileron trim tab
81 Port aileron
82 Port navigation light
83 Pitot head
84 Wing skinning
85 Ammunition loading panels
86 Bead sight
87 Coolant expansion tank, capacity 2.9 Imp gal (13 l)
88 Carburettor intake

103 Curtiss Electric propeller
104 Radiator (divided) intakes
105 Intake trunking
106 Oil cooler radiator
   (centreline)
107 Glycol radiators (port and
   starboard)
108 Radiator mounting brackets
109 Glycol radiator intake pipe
110 Port mainwheel
111 Controllable cooling gills
112 Access panel (oil drain)
113 Engine bearer support truss
114 Fresh air intake
115 Wingroot fairing
116 Fuselage frame/wing
   attachment

117 Walkway
118 Wing/fuselage splice plate
119 Split flap structure
120 Aileron fixed tab
121 Starboard aileron
122 Starboard wingtip
   construction
123 Starboard navigation light
124 Wing rib
125 Multi (7)-spar wing
   structure
126 Inboard gun ammunition
   box (235 rounds)
127 Centre gun ammunition box
   (235 rounds)
128 Outboard gun ammunition
   box (235 rounds)
129 Three 0.50-in (12,7-mm) M-
   2 Browing machine guns
130 Ammunition feed chute

131 Starboard wheel well
132 Wing centre-section main
   fuel tank, capacity 42.1
   Imp gal (191 l)
133 Undercarriage attachment
134 Wing centre-section reserve
   fuel tank, capacity 29.2
   Imp gal (133 l)
135 Retraction cylinder
136 Retraction arm/links
137 Machine gun barrel forward
   support collars
138 Blast tubes
139 Bevel gear
140 Undercarriage side support
   strut
141 Gun warm air
142 500-lb (227-kg) bomb
   (ventral stores)
143 Undercarriage oleo leg
   fairing
144 Undercarriage fairing door

145 Machine gun ports
146 Hydraulic brake line
147 One (or two) underwing 40-
   lb (18-kg) bomb(s)
148 Oleo leg
149 Torque links
150 Axle
151 30-in (76,2-mm) diameter
   smooth-contour
   mainwheel tyre
152 Tow ring/jack point
153 Ventral auxiliary tank,
   capacity 43.3 Imp gal
   (197 l)
154 Vent line
155 Sway brace pads
156 External fuel line
157 Shackle assembly
158 Filler neck
159 Alternative ventral 250-lb
   (113,5-kg) bomb with:
160 Extended percussion fuse

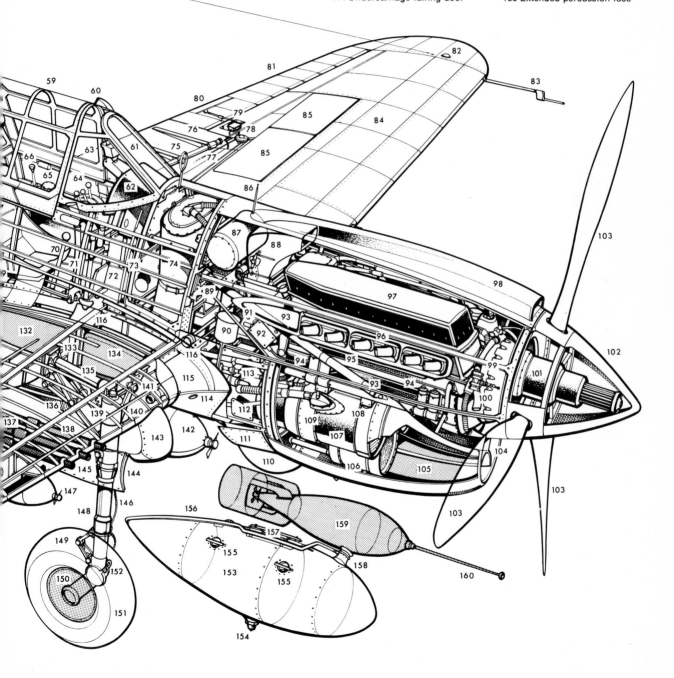

(Above) To help develop an all-round-view cockpit for the P-40Q, this XP-40N was used; production P-40Ns did not incorporate the new feature, however.

Two of the aircraft used in development of the P-40Q: (above), the first XP-40Q with wing-root intakes and the second XP-40Q with revised nose intake and all-round-view cockpit.

fighters built, 5,492 were supplied to Allied nations through Lend-Lease, of which 2,799 were for British Commonwealth countries. The other major recipient of the P-40 series was the Soviet Union, to which nation 2,069 were allocated. Nationalist China received 377 after the formation of the 1st Chinese-American Composite Wing, and Brazil received 89. Details of the other users of the P-40s, Kittyhawks and Warhawks are given later.

Although the majority of the later Warhawks were delivered via Lend-Lease, the USAAF continued to use the type operationally into 1945, principally in the Pacific area but also in the Mediterranean. As already related, P-40Ks eventually entered service with the squadrons of the 23rd FG in the CBI, the Warhawks finally giving way to P-51s in this Group in April 1944. The 51st FG (25th and 26th FS) FG was operating in India by the end of 1942 with P-40s (mostly K models) as part of the US Tenth AF, and in March 1943 China Air Task Force under Chennault became the Fourteenth AF, within which the 1st Chinese-American Composite Wing was formed, having eight squadrons of P-40Ks distributed between its 3rd and 5th Groups. The two squadrons of the 51st FG were also transferred to the Fourteenth, being replaced in June 1943 in India by the 80th FG with three squadrons (88th, 89th and 90th) of P-40s and one (459th) of P-38s.

In the Far North, the USAAF strength in Alaska was built up with the arrival of the 54th Fighter Squadron, joining the 11th and 18th FS already there to form the 343rd FG. In July 1943, the 344th FS was added to the strength of this Group, flying a mixture of P-40Ds, Ks and Ms; the Group flew its last combat mission in October of that year but continued to fly patrol and

Curtiss P-40E-1 Specification
Power Plant: One Allison V-1710-39 12-cylinder Vee liquid-cooled engine with single-speed supercharger, rated at 1,150 hp for take-off and military power at 11,700 ft (3 569 m) and 1,000 hp for continuous operation at 10,800 ft (3 295 m). Curtiss Electric three-blade constant speed propeller, diameter 11 ft 0 in (3,36 m). Fuel capacity, 87 US gal (330 l) in two wing tanks and 62 US gal (235 l) in fuselage plus provision for one 52 US gal (197 l) drop tank.
Performance: Max speed 335 mph (539 km/h) at 5,000 ft (1 525 m) and 362 mph (582 km/h) at 15,000 ft (4 575 m); cruising speed, max continuous power, 296 mph (476 km/h) at 5,000 ft (1 525 m) and 312 mph (502 km/h) at 15,000 ft (4 575 m); time to climb to 5,000 ft (1 525 m), 24 min, to 15,000 ft (4 575 m), 7.6 min and to 25,000 ft (7 625 m), 18.2 min; range (internal fuel), 525 mls (845 km) at max cruise power; range with drop tank, 850 mls (1 368 km) at long range cruise.
Weights: Basic, 6,900 lb (3 133 kg); combat, 8,400 lb (3 814 kg); max take-off, 9,100 lb (4 131 kg).
Dimensions: Span, 37 ft 4 in (11,38 m); length, 31 ft 9 in (9,68 m); height, 12 ft 4 in (3,76 m); undercarriage track, 8 ft 2 in (2,49 m); wing area, 236 sq ft (21,92 m²).
Armament: Six 0.50-in (12,7-mm) machine guns in wings with an average of 281 rpg. Provision under fuselage for one bomb of up to 500-lb (227-kg), and under wings for two 100-lb (45-kg) or six 20-lb (9,1-kg) bombs.

Curtiss P-40F-5 Specification
Power Plant: One Packard V-1650-1 12-cylinder Vee liquid-cooled engine with single-stage two-speed supercharger, rated at 1,300 hp for take-off, and with military ratings of 1,240 hp at 11,500 ft (3 508 m) and 1,120 hp at 18,500 ft (5 643 m). Curtiss Electric three-blade constant speed propeller, diameter 11 ft 0 in (3,36 m). Fuel capacity, 91 US gal (344 l) in two wing tanks and 66 US gal (250 l) in fuselage plus provision for one 52, 75, 150 or 170 US gal (197, 284, 568 or 643 l) drop tank.
Performance: Max speed, 320 mph (515 km/h) at 5,000 ft (1 525 m) and 364 mph (586 km/h) at 20,000 ft (6 100 m); cruising speed, max continuous power, 300 mph (483 km/h) at 5,000 ft (1 525 m) and 332 mph (534 km/h) at 15,000 ft (4 575 m); time to climb to 5,000 ft (1 525 m). 2.4 min to 15,000 ft (4 575 m). 7.6 min and to 25,000 ft (7 625 m), 18.3 min; range (internal fuel), 600 mls (965 km) at max cruise power; range with max external fuel, 1,500 mls (2 414 km) at long range cruise.
Weights: Basic, 7,000 lb (3 178 kg); combat, 8,500 lb (3 860 kg), max take-off, 10,000 lb (4 540 kg).
Dimensions: Span, 37 ft 4 in (11,38 m); length, 33 ft 4 in (10,17 m); height, 12 ft 4 in (3,76 m); undercarriage track, 8 ft 2 in (2,49 m); wing area, 236 sq ft (21,92 m).
Armament: Six 0.50-in (12,7-mm) machine guns in wings with an average of 281 rpg. Provision under fuselage for one bomb of up to 500-lb (227-kg) and under wings for two 100-lb (45-kg) or six 20-lb (9,1-kg) bomb.

reconnaissance sorties in the Aleutian area until the end of the war, with P-38s supplementing the P-40s.

In Australia, the 49th FG equipped with P-40s (having left its P-35s in the USA) to serve with the Fifth AF, its three squadrons (7th, 8th and 9th) having a mixture of P-40Es and Ks. Based in Northern Australia, these squadrons saw considerable combat activity against Japanese bombing attacks, receiving a Distinguished Unit Citation in the process, during 1942, then moving to New Guinea to become engaged primarily in the air defence of Port Moresby. Its squadrons received P-40Ns in 1943 before finally switching to P-38s. Recovering from its mauling in Hawaii, the 18th FG received new P-40s and was back to strength to participate in the Guadalcanal Campaign, flying P-40E, F, M and N versions of the Warhawk. Flying with the Seventh AF, the 15th FG, which had shared the Hawaiian debacle with the 18th, operated P-40s in the island-hopping campaign until the end of 1943, when it received P-51s.

The other principal area of deployment for USAAF Warhawks was the Mediterranean Theatre, the 57th FG

A three-view drawing of the P-40Q as represented by the second XP-40Q, showing the clipped wing tips and revised nose intake.

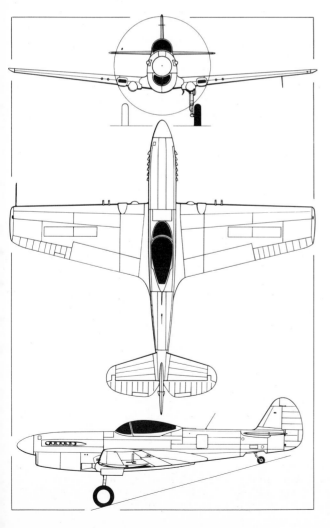

arriving with its 64th, 65th and 66th FS in Palestine in August 1942, flying P-40Fs and P-40Ks The first American victory in operations over the desert was claimed on 9 August when one of these aircraft shot down two Bf 109s. Subsequently transferred from RAF control to the US Ninth AF, the three squadrons of the 57th FG had claimed 20 victories by 4 November, being joined a few days later — for the Operation "Torch" landings in North Afrca — by the P-40Fs of the 33rd FG (58th, 59th and 60th FS) in Morocco and the 79th FG (85th, 86th and 87th FS) in Egypt. Two more P-40 squadrons, the 314th and 316th (part of the 324th FG) reached the Western Desert in December. Pilots of the 65th, 66th and 314th Squadrons participated in what became known as the Palm Sunday Massacre on 18 April 1943, when 47 Warhawks (protected by 12 RAF Spitfires as top cover) intercepted a large formation of *Luftwaffe* Ju 52/3ms attempting to fly supplies in to Rommel's beleaguered forces. The American formation claimed the destruction of 58 Ju 52/3ms, plus 18 escorting Macchi MC 202 and Bf 109 fighters for the loss of four P-40s and a Spitfire, and three pilots of the 57th FG became "instant aces".

Also in April 1943, the 325th FG (317th, 318th and 319th Squadrons) entered action, their P-40Fs distinctively marked with a black and yellow checkerboard pattern, giving this Group its name of the Checkertail Clan. Flying a mixture of strafing and bomber/escort missions, the Checkertail P-40s claimed 135 enemy aircraft destroyed in 128 missions for the loss of 35 aircraft. Flying P-40Ns, the USAAF's unique 99th Fighter Squadron (the personnel of which were all negroes) participated in the North African fighting from April 1943 onwards, and together with the squadrons of the 33rd, 79th and 324th FGs, took P-40s

Curtiss P-40N-1 Specification
Power Plant: One Allison V-1710-81 12-cylinder Vee liquid-cooled engine with single speed supercharger, rated at 1,200 hp for take-off, and with military rating of 1,125 hp at 17,300 ft (5 276 m) and continuous rating of 1,000 hp at 16,400 ft (5 000 m). Curtiss Electric three-bladed constant-speed propeller, diameter 11 ft 0 in (3,36 m). Fuel capacity, one 54 US gal (204 l) tank in wing, one 68 US gal (257 l) tank in fuselage plus provision for one 52, 75, 150 or 170 US gal (197, 284, 568 or 643 l) drop tank.
Performance: Max speed, 313 mph (504 km/h) at 5,000 ft (1 525 m) and 348 mph (560 km/h) at 15,000 ft (4 575 m); rate of climb at 5,000 ft (1 525 m), 2,425 ft/min (40,4 m/sec); time to 5,000 ft (1 525 m), 2.1 min, to 15,000 ft (4 575 m), 6.7 min, to 25,000 ft (7 625 m), 12.4 min; range (internal fuel, 500-lb/227-kg bomb), 420 mls (675 km) at max cruise power; range, max external fuel, 1,250 mls (2 010 km) at long range cruise.
Weights: Basic, 6,400 lb (2 906 kg); combat; 7,725 lb (3 507 kg); max take-off, 8,850 lb (4 018 kg).
Dimensions: Span, 37 ft 4 in (11,38 m); length, 33 ft 4 in (10,17 m); height, 12 ft 4 in (3,76 m); undercarriage track, 8 ft 2 in (2,49 m); wing area, 236 sq ft (21,92 m²).
Armament: Four 0.50-in (12,7-mm) machine guns in wings with average of 201 rpg. Provision under fuselage for one bomb of up to 500-lb (227-kg) and under wings for two 100-lb (45-kg) or six 20-lb (9,1-kg) bombs.

on into Italy before re-equipping with newer types during 1944, flying the Warhawks primarily on ground attack missions.

British Kittyhawks

As already indicated, the Royal Air Force took on charge an initial quantity of 560 Kittyhawk Is, purchased on direct contract, and was then allocated through Lend-Lease 1,500 Kittyhawk IAs (P-40E-1), 330 Kittyhawk IIs (P-40F), 616 Kittyhawk IIIs (21 P-40L and 595 P-40M) and 536 Kittyhawk IV (P-40N). Not all of these were delivered to the RAF, 81 Kittyhawk IIs being retained by the USAAF, some being lost at sea and others being transferred to Commonwealth Air Forces and the Soviet Union; and the great majority of those that did reach British service were delivered direct to North Africa, no operational Kittyhawk squadrons being based in the UK.

The first RAF Kittyhawk squadron was No 112, although its January 1942 debut in the Western Desert was in fact preceded by initial operations by one of the RAAF squadrons, No 3, in the same area. Conversion of Tomahawk squadrons to the newer type proceeded rapidly and Nos 260, 250 and 94 Squadrons, RAF, were flying the Mk I by February 1942. Of these four RAF units, No 94 converted to Hurricanes in May 1942, Nos 112 and 260 flew successive marks of Kittyhawk (except

the Mk II) until July and March 1944 respectively and No 250 retained Kittyhawk IVs until May 1945.

Commanded by Sqdn Ldr Clive "Killer" Caldwell, No 112 Squadron adapted its Kittyhawks to carry 250-lb (114-kg) bombs and began an intensive period of operations combining strafing and ground attack with bomber escort duties, some pilots making three or four sorties per day. Similar duties were performed by the other Kittyhawk squadrons, the soubriquet Kitty-bomber being coined at this time, and Nos 112, 250 and 260 saw action continuously throughout the campaign in Italy.

Australian Kittyhawks

The first RAAF use of P-40s in Australia occurred in March 1942 at short notice, when an urgent need arose to provide fighter defence for Port Moresby, New Guinea, where a squadron of Hudsons and six Catalinas were based, without protection. Twenty-five P-40Es were transferred by the USAAF to the RAAF in Australia, and these were used to equip No 75 Squadron, which formed for the purpose at Townsville on 4 March. After a brief working up period, this unit moved to Port Moresby on 19 March, by way of Cooktown and Horn Island, claiming their first victory on the 21st with destruction of a Japanese bomber on a reconnaissance flight. The squadron became heavily engaged on a daily basis almost as soon as it arrived, and by 30 April had only three serviceable P-40Es left; two of these were lost on 2 May, but three more were made airworthy, two of these in turn being shot up on the ground on 9 May. In 44 days at Port Moresby, No 75 Squadron claimed the destruction of 35 aircraft plus four probables and 47 damaged for the loss of 12 pilots and 22 P-40s.

The next Curtiss fighters to reach the RAAF — and all its future Kittyhawks — were Lend-Lease supplies diverted from the British allocations, and comprised

In service with the RAF, Curtiss Kittyhawks were deployed principally in the Middle East, serving notably in the African campaign. A typical desert take-off by a bomb-carrying Kittyhawk I sporting the shark's teeth marking of No 112 Squadron is shown below and a long-fuselage Kittyhawk IV is illustrated above.

During 1943, the RAAF made available 95 Kittyhawk IVs (P-40Ns) to the Dutch government to equip No 120 Squadron of the Royal Netherlands Indies Army Air Force; three of its aircraft are shown (above) operating in 1944 from Biak, New Guinea. (Below) One of the RAAF's Kittyhawk IAs in flight over New South Wales in 1942.

139 Kittyhawk IAs. These were used to bring No 75 Squadron back to strength, and then, progressively, to equip additional squadrons — Nos 76, 77, 78, 80, 82, 84 and 86. No 76 joined No 75 in New Guinea in August, and shared in the fighting that eventually forced the Japanese evacuation of its forces in the Milne Bay area at the eastern extremity of the island. The respite was only a brief one, however, and Nos 76, 76 and 77 Squadrons were soon in action again as the battle to push other Japanese forces out of Papua and New Guinea intensified. During 1943, the additional Kittyhawk squadrons joined the fight in the SW Pacific, and they flew combat missions right up to the end of hostilities, attacking a target in Borneo on 23 July 1945. Initially flying purely as defensive fighters, they later went over to the offensive, flying as bomber escorts and on ground attack missions carrying bombs. The strength of the RAAF Kittyhawk squadrons was kept up by the allocation of 42 P-40Ks, 90 P-40Ms and 546 P-40Ns.

RAAF units also flew Kittyhawks in the Western Desert, where No 3 Squadron (RAAF) was in fact the first unit to operate the Kittyhawk I, to which it converted from the Tomahawk II in December 1941, becoming operational again on the 30th of that month. No 450 Squadron (RAAF), one of the so-called "infiltration" squadrons formed by mixing Australian personnel with an RAF unit (in this case No 260 Squadron) for a period of indoctrination before hiving off the new unit, equipped on Kittyhawks in February 1942, and these two units operated with the RAF Kittyhawk squadrons through North Africa and into Italy. Unlike the Kittyhawks used by RAAF Squadrons in the Pacific, which carried Australian serial numbers with the A29 prefix, those used by the two squadrons in the Mediterranean theatre retained RAF serial numbers.

The RAAF also made available facilities in Australia for the formation of a Kittyhawk squadron manned by Dutch personnel. The pilots for this unit, No 120 Squadron, were trained at a joint Dutch Army-Navy flying school at Jackson, Missouri, established after the collapse of resistance in both the Netherlands and the

East Indies; of some 334 aircrew trained at Jackson, 67 were assigned as fighter pilots and from these were drawn the members of No 120 Squadron, for the use of which a total of 67 P-40Ns was made available from USAAF stocks through Lend-Lease. After working up in Australia from December 1943 on, this unit became operational alongside RAAF units flying in the SW Pacific area and in June 1945 it was transferred to the revived Royal Netherlands Indies Army Air force in Java.

South African Kittyhawks

Sharing the fighting in the Western Desert with the RAF and RAAF Squadrons were two units of the South African Air Force, both of which converted from Tomahawks to Kittyhawk IAs in June 1942. At the same time, No 10 Squadron started using Kittyhawks at Durban, serving as an advanced training and conversion unit to supply pilots to the operational squadrons. In January 1943, No 5 Squadron, also in the Western Desert, began flying Kittyhawk IAs and these units flew successive marks, made available from RAF Lend-Lease supplies, until late in the war. They were joined by a fourth operational Kittyhawk squadron in November 1944, this being No 11 which converted in Italy from Spitfires, for ground-attack duties.

New Zealand Kittyhawks

To help New Zealand expand her fighter defences and — in the longer term — participate in the fighting in the Pacific alongside Australian and US forces, Britain agreed to release 62 Kittyhawk Is to the RNZAF, these arriving in July and August 1942. These aircraft were used to equip Nos 14, 15 and 16 Squadrons, of which the first-mentioned was formed from the nucleus of No 488 Squadron, a Buffalo-equipped unit that had been severely mauled in the fighting for Malaya and the Netherlands East Indies earlier in the year. No 15 Squadron was despatched, without aircraft, to Tonga in October 1942 where it took over the 23 P-40Ks of the USAAF's 68th PS and maintained the defence of the area for 3 months, without seeing any action.

It remained to No 14 Squadron, therefore, to take the RNZAF Kittyhawks into action, when that unit moved to Santo Island in April 1943 to take over its defence from the Americans. A batch of 35 P-40Ms plus a single P-40L was made available for this purpose, and subsequently 172 P-40Ns were supplied to bring the total of RNZAF Kittyhawks to 293. Progressively, Nos 15 and 16 Squadrons entered the combat zone, flying alongside USAAF units in defence of the Solomons, and flying patrols, interceptions and bomber escort duties which exacted a steady toll of squadron pilots whilst allowing only modest successes in terms of combat victories. A fourth squadron, No 17, was formed in New Zealand in October 1942 and this unit took its turn in the front-line, allowing the other squadrons to stand-down in rotation.

During 1943, Nos 18 and 19 Squadrons formed on Kittyhawks, followed by No 20 in January 1944, but the last-mentioned converted to Corsairs before it entered

(Above) With bombs under the fuselage and both wings, a Kittyhawk I is guided from its dispersal at a forward air base by a ground crewman sitting on the port wing. (Below) Four Kittyhawk IAs of No 16 Squadron, RNZAF, in training prior to its departure for action in the New Hebrides.

combat, and the Curtiss fighter began to be phased out of the other New Zealand units in the next few weeks. By February 1944, the RNZAF Kittyhawk squadrons had claimed a total of 99 Japanese aircraft destroyed — the 100th victory proving impossible to achieve before the squadrons re-equipped.

Canadian Kittyhawks

Britain diverted 72 of its direct-purchase Kittyhawk Is to Canada for use by the RCAF, the intention being to equip a number of squadrons to provide a defensive force within Canada. Deliveries, direct from the Curtiss plant in Buffalo, began in October 1941, the squadrons equipped with the type being Nos 14, 111 and 118 and Nos 130, 132 and 133 also flying the Kittyhawk Is later. First to equip was No 118 Squadron, starting in late October 1941 when it was flying CCF-built Grumman Goblin Is and Hurricanes.

Late in May 1942, the US government had requested Canadian assistance in the defence of Alaska, with the result that No 111 Squadron (its Kittyhawks still bearing RAF serial numbers — replaced a year later by RCAF serials) was despatched immediately to Yakutat in Southern Alaska, flying on to Elmendorf Field, Anchorage, on 5 June — the same day that Japanese forces attacked Dutch Harbor. The squadron saw no action then, but was moved up to Umnak, the most distant base in the Aleutians, in July. While nine pilots flew up in a transport, seven others followed in Kittyhawks, but two of these were lost on the first leg to Naknek and, after replacements were flown in from Elmendorf, five of the seven crashed *en route* to Cold Bay. The Canadian pilots then formed "F" Flight of the USAAF's 11th PS at Umnak, flying P-40Es until nine USAAF P-40K-1s were acquired as replacement aircraft in August 1942. (These operated in RCAF markings but with USAAF serials and were handed back in June 1943). Participating in the first American strike on Japanese forces occupying Kiska, four P-40Ks intercepted a Nakajima A6M2-N ("Rufe") floatplane and it was shot down by the CO of No 111 Squadron, Sqdn Ldr K Boomer, this being the only Japanese aircraft destroyed by a Canadian aircraft flying from the North American mainland during World War II.

No 14 Squadron, also with Kittyhawk Is, flew to Alaska in January 1943, flying from Umnak for a time, replacing No 111 which had moved to Kodiak in October 1942, on defensive patrols and training sorties. The latter unit moved up to Amchitka in May 1943 and for two months flew ground attack sorties against Japanese forces occupying Kiska, in which No 14 Squadron also participated. These units returned to Canada in September and August respectively. Between June 1942 and 1943, No 118 Squadron, with its Kittyhawk Is, was based at Annette Island, flying in defence of Southern Alaska and the Prince Rubert area of BC.

In 1942, 12 Kittyhawk IAs were supplied to Canada, primarily being used by No 132(F) Squadron. Fifteen Kittyhawk IIIs (P-40M) and 35 Kittyhawk IVs (P-40N)

Kittyhawk IA serial 729 was one of 12 supplied to the RCAF in 1942 and used primarily by No 132(F) Squadron. The RCAF also operated the Kittyhawk I, III, and IV.

were similarly diverted from RAF supplies to Canada in 1943 and 1944, these aircraft being used by Western Air Command and by Nos 132 and 135 Squadrons.

French Warhawks

Although Hawk 75A-4s of the French GC II/5 fought vigorously against US forces engaged in the Operation "Torch" landings in North Africa in November 1942, within two weeks this same unit had been issued with P-40F Warhawks in order to fight alongside the Allies. The step was taken with some misgivings on the part of the Allied commanders, and not without reason, for two of GC II/5's pilots defected to German-occupied Southern France on their first operation with P-40s! However, this lapse apart, the *Groupe* fought with tenacity during the Tunisian campaigns in 1943, receiving P-47s in place of the P-40s at the end of that year.

Sentiment played a part in making this particular episode possible, for GC II/5 was the *Escadrille Lafayette*, its Hawk 75A-4s bearing the Sioux Indian head insignia that had been first carried by the squadrons of volunteer American pilots in France in World War I. The sight of this famous marking on the Hawks in North Africa inspired a group of USAAF officers, at least one of whom had flown in the original squadron, to press for the *Groupe* to be given the opportunity to fight alongside the Americans again — and to this end, 25 long-fuselage P-40F Warhawks were issued to the unit at Casablanca on 25 November 1942. On 24 December, the unit was officially designated the *Groupe Lafayette* and on 9 January, 13 of the P-40s flew to Tunisia (two defecting *en route*) to serve as part of the 33rd Fighter Group in the USAAF. Operating from Thelepte, where 12 more P-40s arrived on 17 January, the *Groupe* achieved its first success on the 10th, shooting down two Ju 88s.

When the airfield was overrun by German forces in Rommel's sudden offensive in Tunisia in mid-February, only 16 Warhawks could be evacuated; these resumed operations on 20 February from Kalaa-Djerba but another evacuation was necessary, two more P-40s being lost *en route*, and when the *Groupe* finally returned to Morocco on 15 March, only five remained flyable, although only six of the 20 losses were attributable to direct enemy action. The squadron was credited with seven confirmed victories up to this time, in 287 sorties.

Re-equipment took the form of 36 P-40Ls, which the *Groupe Lafayette* took back to Tunisia in May 1943 with four P-40Fs. These were used for coastal patrols and air defence until December, when the *Groupe* re-equipped. A few P-40s continued in service, however, at training bases in Morocco and some of the survivors were used to the end of the war and beyond at the Mont-de-Marsan base in SW France.

P-40Fs of the Groupe Lafayette *lined up for official ceremony at Casablanca before flying to Tunisia on 9 January 1943. This famous unit suffered heavy losses in the first three months of P-40 operation, later receiving P-40Ls as replacements.*

Curtiss XP-46

By its development of the P-40 (see page 48), the Aeroplane Division of Curtiss-Wright Corporation had maintained its leading position among fighter designers in the USA by 1939, but a study of fighters already in service in Europe led the company to conclude that a number of desirable features had been omitted from the P-40 design. Proposals were therefore made to the US Army Air Corps for a potential successor to the P-40 incorporating such "European" features as a wide-track undercarriage, automatic leading-edge slots to assist manoeuvering near the stall and a baattery of eight machine guns in the wings.

An Air Corps specification was written round the Curtiss proposal and on 29 September 1939 two prototypes of this new fighter were ordered, the designation XP-46 being assigned. Its design was generaly similar to that of the P-40, but the overall

A side view (top) of the XP-46A and three-view drawing of the XP-46.

(Above) The sole Curtiss XP-46 and (below) the unarmed XP-46A which was the first to fly.

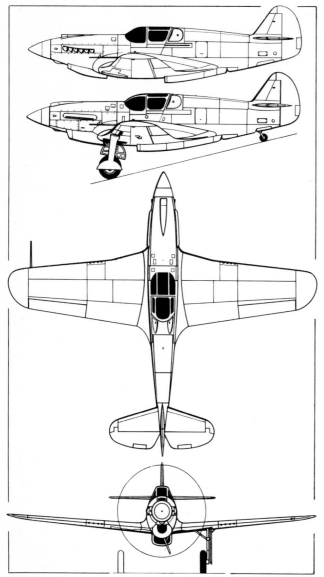

dimensions were considerably smaller; the engine was the 1,150 hp Allison V-1710-39 and with a gross weight of 6,849 lb (3 19 kg), a top speed of 410 mph (660 km/h) at 15,000 ft (4 575 m) was predicted. During construction, however, the XP-46 suffered considerable weight growth — partly as a result of the Air Corps adding a requirement for self-sealing fuel tanks and 65 lb (29,5 kg) of armour protection — and the performance of the aircraft never came up to expectation.

First flight of the new fighter was made on 15 February 1941, this being the unarmed second aircraft, designated XP-46A; it was delivered to the Air Corps on 12 September, followed by the XP-46 on 22 September. Several months earlier, Curtiss and the Army Air Corps had come to the conclusion that the performance of the XP-46 could most probably be matched by using the same F3R version of the Allison V-1710 in the P-40 airframe, albeit producing a somewhat less tractable and less heavily armed fighter, but one that could be produced without interruption of the production line already functioning. Consequently, the P-46 was replaced in forward planning by the P-40D with the V-1710-39 which, in due course, was demonstrated to have a superior performance, and the former type was soon dropped completely.

Curtiss XP-46 Specification
Power Plant: One 1,150 hp Allison V-1710-39 (F3R) 12-cylinder Vee in-line liquid-cooled engine.
Performance: Max speed, 355 mph (571 km/h) at 12,200 ft (3 721 m); max cruising speed, 332 mph (534 km/h); time to 12,300 ft (3 752 m); 5 min; service ceiling, 29,500 ft (8 997 m); range at max cruise, 325 mls (523 km).
Weights: Empty, 5,625 lb (2 554 kg); normal loaded, 7,322 lb (3 324 kg); max take-off, 7,665 lb (3 480 kg).
Dimensions: Span, 34 ft 4 in (10,47 m); length, 30 ft 2 in (9,19 m); height, 13 ft 0 in (3,97 m); wing area, 208 sq ft (19,32 m²).
Armament: Two 0.50-in (12,7-mm) machine guns in upper forward fuselage decking and eight 0.30-in (7,7-mm) machine guns in wings.

The unorthodox Curtiss Ascender resulted from a USAAF initiative intended to free fighter designers from customary restraints in the hope that improved performance would result from a radical approach. It did not.

CURTISS XP-55 ASCENDER

As part of the constant quest for better performance in combat aeroplanes, the US Army Air Corps drew up, during 1939, a highly challenging specification for a new fighter. Whilst the development of single-engined pursuit types had been progressing along conventional lines with the gradual acceptance of monoplane configurations, stressed skin construction, variable-pitch propellers and retractable undercarriages, in company with increased engine power and heavier armament, it was believed in some circles that a more radical approach to fighter design might pay dividends. Specification XC-622, issued on 27 November 1939, therefore set forth very stringent performance requirements and, by calling for the use of the relatively low-powered Pratt & Whitney X-1800-AG engine, placed a premium upon low overall drag. Special attention was also demanded for pilot visibility and the armament installation.

Three companies — Curtiss Aeroplane Division of Curtiss-Wright Corp, Vultee Aircraft Inc and Northrop Aircraft Inc — responded to the invitation to submit design proposals and in due course prototypes of all three designs were built; each was radical in concept, but the most unconventional of the trio was the Curtiss Model 24 Ascender. Placed second in the evaluations of the project designs, the Curtiss proposal was for an aircraft combining characteristics of the flying wing and the tail-first canard type, without being a true representative of either of these configurations: essentially, it was a flying wing type with a controllable nose elevator.

Action to procure preliminary engineering data and a powered wind tunnel model was initiated by the Army on 31 May 1940, backed up by a contract dated 22 June 1940. The ¼-scale powered wind tunnel model, constructed almost entirely of aluminium alloy and weighing 600 lb (272 kg), was tested in the Wright Brothers tunnel at the Massachusetts Institute of Technology from 5 November 1940 onwards, more than 500 separate runs being made, with two separate wings using NACA aerofoils (one conventional and one laminar flow); later, the studies were extended to embrace a North American section and some Curtiss-Wright sections, and eventually the CW6500-0015 laminar flow aerofoil was selected. Simultaneously, a $1/16$th-scale spin model was tested by NACA, and indicated that the spin characteristics were questionable.

With changing tactical requirements and the wind tunnel tests not completely satisfactory, Army interest in the Curtiss project began to wane, and an option to proceed to mock-up construction and purchase of a flying prototype was dropped. Curtiss-Wright then decided to finance the construction of a low-powered, full-scale flying model to keep the project alive. Identified as the Model 24-B, this flying model was completed in the autumn of 1941 and shortly before it was ready to fly, Army interest revived, a contract being issued to cover its flight testing at the Muroc Bombing Range (later, Edwards AFB) in California. Powered by a 275 hp Menasco C68-5 engine, the Model 24-B had a welded-tube fuselage structure with fabric covering, and a wooden wing; the undercarriage was fixed but in most other respects the aircraft was aerodynamically representative of the planned fighter.

Between November 1941 and May 1942, the Model

The Curtiss CW-24B was a full-scale low-powered lightweight model of the XP-55, built to prove the soundness of the configuration.

Curtiss XP-55 Specification

Power Plant: One Allison V-1710-95 liquid-cooled 12-cylinder Vee engine rated at 1,275 hp for take-off at sea level and 1,125 hp in military rating at 15,500 ft (4 728 m). Curtiss Electric three-bladed propeller, diameter 10 ft (3,05 m). Fuel capacity, 110 US gal (416 l) in internal self-sealing tanks and provision for two 50 US gal (189 l) drop tanks.
Performance: Max speed, 377.5 mph (607 km/h) at 16,900 ft (5 155 m); initial rate of climb, 2,350 ft/min (11,9 m/sec); service ceiling, 35,800 ft (10 920 m); time to 29,155 ft (8 892 m), 16.5 min; take-off distance to 50 ft (15,2 m), 5,000 ft (1 525 m); landing distance from 50 ft (15,2 m), 3,000 ft (915 m); normal range, 635 mls (1 020 km) at 296 mph (476 km/h); max range, 1,440 mls (2 317 km).
Weights: Empty, 6,354 lb (2 884 kg); design useful load, 1,578 lb (716 kg); max take-off, 7,930 lb (3 600 kg).
Dimensions: Span, 41 ft 0 in (12,50 m); length, 29 ft 7 in (9,02 m); height, 10 ft 0¾ in (3,07 m); wing area, 235 sq ft (21,83 m²); dihedral, 4½ deg; wheelbase, 14 ft 0½ in (4,28 m); undercarriage track, 11 ft 10 in (3,61 m).
Armament: Four 0.50-in (12,7-mm) Colt-Browning M-2 machine guns with 200 rpg.

24-B made a total of 169 flights at Muroc, in two phases — first, to arrive at the configuration for optimum flying qualities and then to obtain performance data. In the first phase, end-plate fins were added at the wing tips, then fins *and* rudders were fitted; fins were added to the top and bottom of the engine cowling, and eventually wing tip extensions were fitted beyond the fins and rudders. Some stalling tests were made, showing good control and recovery, but the low-powered model was considered unsafe for spinning trials to be attempted. To improve manoeuvrability, the nose elevator area was increased by 25 per cent during the test programme at Muroc, upon the conclusion of which the Model 24-B underwent full scale wind tunnel testing at Langley.

In April 1942, encouraged by the flight test results, the USAAF began procurement of three prototypes of the Curtiss Model 24, to be designated XP-55 and ordered on 10 July 1942. As the X-1800 engine was not available, these were to be powered by the Allison V-1710-F16 driving a pusher three-bladed propeller (a contra-prop had been proposed in the original submission) and the armament was to comprise two 20-mm cannon and two 0.50-in (12,7-mm) machine guns. After mock-up inspection in the latter months of 1942, the armament was changed to four 0.50-in (12,7-mm) guns and because of availability, the engine variant actually selected for installation was the unsupercharged V-1710-F23R.

The XP-55 was of all-metal stressed-skin construction and had an electrically-actuated retractable undercarriage. Ailerons and nose elevators (with a leading-edge continuous through the fuselage) were actuated by push-pull tubes and the rudders by cable; each elevator half incorporated an all-metal tab and balance tabs were fitted in the ailerons. The four machine guns were grouped in the extreme nose with 200 rpg. Split flaps were fitted to the wing.

Flight testing of the first XP-55 began immediately after its delivery to the SAAF on 13 July 1943 and early

The first of the three prototypes of the XP-55 built under USAAF contract. In the course of flight testing, numerous changes were made to the size and operation of the noseplane.

modifications included a 15 per cent increase in elevator area and an interconnection to give aileron-up trim when flaps were lowered. This prototype was lost on 15 November 1943 when stalling tests were in progress, with wing spoilers fitted; following one stall, the aircraft pitched nose down and continued through 180 deg to enter a stable inverted spin from which recovery proved impossible — partly, at least, because the stall had been entered power-off and an inverted fuel system was not fitted. The pilot escaped by parachute. As a result of subsequent wind tunnel investigations, the third prototype was fitted with wing tip extensions of increased area, but the second XP-55, flown on 9 January 1944, retained essentially the same configuration as the first with the exception of a further small increase in nose elevator area, modified elevator tab system and spring tabs in place of balance tabs on the ailerons.

Before the third XP-55 flew, on 25 April 1944, ground gun firing tests were made. This aircraft had the extended wing tips with "trailerons" fitted, and increased elevator limits, although the latter proved a mixed blessing as it allowed the pilot to stall the elevator during take-off, thus extending the run excessively, and the system was modified in due course. In stalling tests, the third XP-55 proved entirely satisfactory but there was a complete absence of stall warning and a stick shaker was therefore added. The second XP-55 was brought up to the same standard as the third and was used for a series of official performance flights from 16 September to 2 October 1944 and was then delivered to Wright Field for further tests but the blast tubes failed during ground firing and interest in the XP-35 quickly faded. Officially, excessive take-off run and poor stalling characteristics were noted as the main objections to the XP-55, but by the end of 1944 the progress of the war and the evolution of less unconventional fighters of much greater potential had in fact rendered the Curtiss Ascender something of an anachronism.

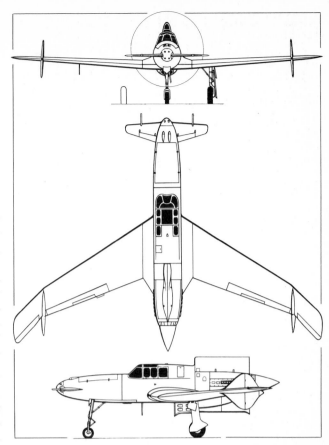

(Top left) A three-view drawing of the Curtiss XP-55 in its final form. (Above left) A ground view of the third prototype and (below) the first prototype in flight.

(Above and below left) Two views of the Curtiss XP-60. Based on the P-40 airframe, it differed primarily in having a Merlin engine and inward instead of rearward retracting undercarriage.

CURTISS P-60

Between 1940 and 1944, Curtiss-Wright and the USAAF expended considerable effort on a series of prototype fighters in the P-60 designation series, as part of an attempt to provide a successor for the P-40. The attempt proved unsuccessful and the P-40 remained the last Curtiss fighter to serve in quantity, but the five P-60 airframes provided an interesting illustration of the way in which a single design could be developed in several different ways, ending up far removed from the starting point.

So far as the P-60 was concerned, that starting point, as noted, was the P-40 which, in 1940, was in production as the most significant new fighter for Army Air Corps units that were still in the early phases of modernisation. Among several proposals made by Curtiss to improve the P-40 was the installation of a 1,250 hp Continental XIV-1430-3 inverted-Vee engine, coupled with a new wing using an NACA laminar-flow aerofoil section and carrying an armament of eight 0.50-in (12,7-mm) machine guns. On 1 October 1940, the Army accepted Curtiss proposals and ordered two prototypes with the designation XP-53. With a gross

weight of 10,603 lb (4 814 kg), the XP-53 was expected to reach 450 mph (724 km/h) at 20,000 ft (6 100 m).

Only six weeks after the XP-53s were ordered, the Army decided to encourage development of a Curtiss fighter with a Rolls-Royce Merlin engine that Packard would build eventually in the USA, and as the Continental XIV-1430 engine was still in its early stages, a contract change was authorised for the second XP-53 to be completed as the XP-60 with an imported Merlin 28. The original P-40-style rearwards-retracting undercarriage was also to be changed to an inward-folding type, totally enclosed when retracted.

While work on the initial XP-53 slowed and was eventually abandoned — the incomplete airframe being used for static testing — the XP-60 proceeded rapidly, flying for the first time on 18 September 1941. Armament, self-sealing fuel tanks and pilot armour were omitted to get the aircraft airborne as rapidly as possible; with the Merlin giving 1,300 hp at take-off and 1,120 hp at 18,500 ft (5 643 m), the XP-60 achieved 380 mph (611 km/h) at 20,000 ft (6 100 m), climbed to 15,000 ft (4 575 m) in 7.3 min and had a range of 995 mls (1 600 km) on max fuel. The gross weight was 9,700 lb (4 404 kg).

With the Packard Merlin production line still to be established and demands for the British engine growing on all sides, Curtiss was constrained to seek alternative engines and proposed the installation of the turbo-supercharged Allison V-1710-75 with a rating of 1,425 hp at 25,000 ft (7 625 m). There were two superchargers available for this engine — the General Electric B-14 and the Wright SU-504-2, and both were put forward as suitable for use in the P-60; a third alternative was the use of the Chrysler XIV-2220, whilst yet another was to fit the Merlin 61 with its two-speed two-stage supercharger. These four alternatives received the respective designations XP-60A, XP-60B, XP-60C and XP-60D, and on 31 October 1941, a production contract for 1,950 P-60As was approved, with B-14 turbo-superchargers on the V-1710-75 engines. However, the XP-60 was not performing faultlessly, and doubts emerged as to the ability of the P-60A to meet its specified performance; consequently, when the attack on Pearl Harbor in December 1941 led the Army to call for a concentration on proven types already in production, the P-60A was a prime candidate for cancellation, and on 20 December the programme was cancelled. In its place, Curtiss received contracts for 1,400 more P-40s and 2,400 P-47 Thunderbolts, and in January 1942 single prototypes of the XP-60A, XP-60B, XP-60C and XP-60D were authorised for completion; of these, the last-mentioned was to be the original XP-60 fitted with Merlin 61 and taller fin and rudder, whilst the other three would be assembled from components produced for the P-60A production.

Completed in October 1942, the XP-60A made its first flight on 1 November, but only after the GE B-14 turbo-supercharger had ben removed because it overheated during ground running. With armament reduced to six 0.50-in (12,7-mm) guns from the original eight, the XP-60A had a gross weight of 9,616 lb (4 366 kg) and a projected top speed of 420 mph (676 km/h) at 29,000 ft (8 845 m). Interest was by this time centred, however, upon a new Curtiss proposal to use the Pratt & Whitney R-2800 engine with two-stage supercharger and six-blade propeller in the XP-60C, instead of the unproven Chrysler engine, and in November 1942 the USAAF took the first steps to order 500 P-60As with this engine. The XP-60C was completed to this new standard, flying for the first time

Curtiss XP-60A Specification

Power Plant: One Allison V-1710-75 liquid-cooled 12-cylinder Vee engine with General Electric B-14 turbo-supercharger. Curtiss Electric four-bladed propeller, diameter 11 ft 8 in (3,56 m). Fuel capacity, 200 US gal (757 l) in self-sealing wing tanks.
Performance: Max speed, 420 mph (676 km/h) at 29,000 ft (6 100 m), 324 mph (521 km/h) at sea level; normal operating speed, 300 mph (483 km/h) at 15,000 ft (4 575 m); initial rate of climb, 2,560 ft/min (13,01 m/sec); time to reach 25,000 ft (7 625 m), 12,4 min; service ceiling, 35,200 ft (10 736 m); take-off distance to 50 ft (15,2 m), 2,200 ft (671 m); landing distance from 50 ft (15,2 m), 2,100 ft (641 m); endurance, 1 hr at normal power with 116 US gal (439 l) of fuel.
Weights: Empty, 7,806 lb (3 544 kg); deisgn useful load, 1,810 lb (822 kg); design gross weight, 9,616 lb (4 366 kg).
Dimensions: Span, 41 ft 3¾ in (12,59 m); length, 33 ft 7½ in (10,26 m); overall height, 12 ft 4 in (3,77 m); wing area, 275.15 sq ft (25,56 m²); dihedral 7 deg constant; undercarriage track, 12 ft 0 in (3,67 m); wheelbase, 19 ft 6 in (5,97 m).
Armament: Six 0.50-in (12,7-mm) machine guns in wing with 200 rpg.

(Above right) Another view of the XP-60, which was subsequently modified to XP-60D with an uprated Merlin and (below) the sole XP-60A, intended to have a turbo-supercharger on its Allison V-1710 engine, but flown without this feature.

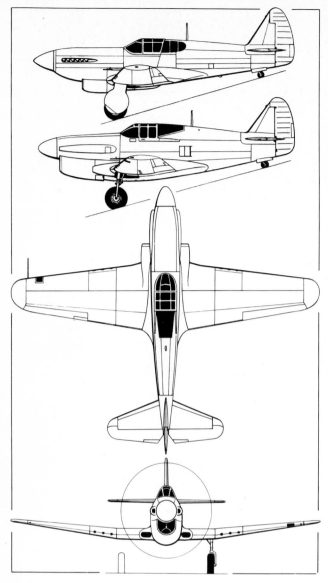

The topmost side view in the drawing above depicts the XP-60 and the three-view shows the XP-60A.

on 27 January 1943, and the USAAF directed that the XP-60B should be abandoned, the incompleted airframe being finished as the XP-60E with an R-2800-10 engine and four-bladed propeller, in case the contraprop installation in the XP-60C gave trouble.

The XP-60E, which had the engine set 10 in (25,4 cm) farther forward than in the XP-60C to compensate for the lighter propeller and lack of gearing, was completed too late to participate in a comparative fighter evaluation conducted by USAAF pilots at Patterson Field at the end of April 1943. Consequently, the XP-60C was submitted, at short notice and in far from optimum condition; a leak in the induction system prevented maximum engine power from being obtained and cracking of the wing leading edge finish destroyed the laminar flow characteristics, with further loss of speed. The tests were terminated prematurely when part of the spinner broke away in flight and damaged the engine cowling.

The XP-60E made its first flight on 26 May 1943 but was seriously damaged in a forced landing following engine failure on 14 August. As testing of the XP-60C, with the contra-prop, was then complete, the engine/propeller combination from the XP-60E was then installed in the XP-60C airframe so that testing of the single propeller could continue, and the designations of the two aircraft were transposed. The original XP-60E airframe was then repaired using the wings, undercarriage and other items from the XP-60A and resumed flight testing as the XP-60C (with contra-prop) in 1944.

The new XP-60E suffered a forced landing on 18 September 1943 through shortage of fuel but was flying again a month later and participated in a fighter conference at Eglin Field in January 1944 before being submitted to official USAAF tests from 1 March to 23 March 1944. After formal acceptance by the Army on 5 June 1944, both the XP-60C and XP-60E were assigned to propeller development.

Work had been going on, early in 1943, on an initial batch of 26 P-60As with R-2800 engines, and full-scale engineering and tooling was under way, but on 3 June 1943 the entire contract was cancelled. Curtiss proposed, and the USAAF agreed, that the first two airframes should be completed for further test work and these were eventually specified as YP-60Es. They differed from the XP-60E in having a raised pilot's seat and a bubble type canopy; redesigned engine cowling and R-2800-18 engine with revised intercooler position and internal fuel capacity raised to 368 US gal (1 393 l). Work on these aircraft proceeded only slowly, and by May 1944, Curtiss was anxious to end all further work on the P-60. USAAF insisted, however, upon completion of one of the two YP-60Es, which eventually flew on 13 July 1944. It was delivered to Wright Field after only two flights and no further testing was undertaken by the USAAF; thus the saga of the P-60 came, officially, to an end.

Unexpectedly, the YP-60E re-appeared briefly in 1947 — in civil guise as NX21979 *Connie II* — as a competitor in the Thompson Trophy event at the Cleveland National Air Races. In an attempt to boost

The Curtiss XP-60C was distinguished by its R-2800 engine and counter-rotating propeller. After this prototype had completed testing, it became an XP-60E with single-rotating propeller, and the contra-prop was transferred to the original XP-60E airframe, which then became known as XP-60C.

(Above) The single YP-60E, representing the definitive form of the P-60 series as finally approved for production but ultimately abandoned. (Below left) the XP-60E — actually the original XP-60C with a single-rotation propeller. (Below right) A side view of the XP-60C and three views of the YP-60E, with a longer nose and all-round vision cockpit.

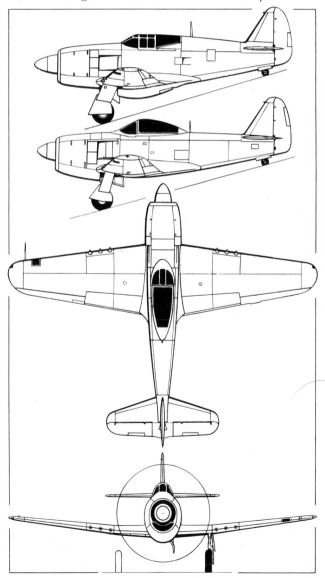

the YP-60E's speed from the Curtiss estimate of 420 mph (676 km/h) to a possible 450 mph (724 km/h), the new owner James De Santo had clipped 10 ft 2 in (3,10 m) from the wing span and had hotted up the engine to give 2,400 hp, but the prototype's potential was never proved for it suffered structural failure of the tail unit during an aerobatic display prior to the race and was destroyed, De Santo bailing out to safety.

Curtiss XP-60E Specification

Power Plant: One Pratt & Whitney R-2800-10 air-cooled 14-cylinder two-row radial engine rated at 2,000 hp for take-off and 1,650 hp at military rating at 22,500 ft (6 863 m). Curtiss Electric four-blade propeller, diameter 13 ft 0 in (3,97 m). Max fuel capacity, 225 US gal (852 l).
Performance: Max speed, 410 mph (186 km/h) at 20,200 ft (6 160 m); cruising speed, 348 mph (158 km/h) at 17,500 ft (5 338 m); initial rate of climb, 4,200 ft/min (21,35 m/sec); take-off distance to 50 ft (15,2 m), 1,265 ft (386 m); endurance, ¾-hr at 391 mph (178 km/h) on 178 US gal (674 l).
Weights: Empty, 8,574 lb (3 893 kg); design useful load, 2,093 lb (950 kg) design gross weight, 10,677 lb (4 843 kg).
Dimensions: Span, 41 ft 3¾ in (12,59 m); length, 33 ft 11 in (10,34 m); height, 12 ft 6 in (3,81 m); wing area, 275.15 sq ft (25,56 m²); dihedral, 7½ deg constant; undercarriage track, 12 ft 0   in (3,67 m); wheelbase, 21 ft 6¾ in (6,57 m).
Armament: Four 0.50-in (12,7-mm) machine guns in wing, with 250 rpg.

Curtiss XP-62

When the Curtiss company was invited by the USAAC, in January 1941, to design a high-performance fighter around a new Wright 18-cylinder engine, a number of innovations was specified, including the use of a pressure cabin, a very heavy armament, contra-prop and an exhaust-driven supercharger. The engine was to be the R-3350, which with a rating of 2,250 hp was then the most powerful engine under development in the USA for aircraft use.

Undaunted by the technical challenges inherent in the USAAF requirement, Curtiss proposed, in April 1941, to design and deliver, within 18 months, two prototypes of such a fighter with an armament of eight 20-mm or twelve 0.50-in (12,7-mm) guns and a top speed of 468 mph (753 km/h) at 27,000 ft (8 235 m). A contract was approved on 27 June 1941 for the two aircraft, one to be designated XP-62 and one XP-62A. The specification was later revised to promise only 448 mph (721 km/h) with the eight-cannon armament, because of weight growth, but the USAAF still regarded this as most satisfactory; a few months later, a major attempt was initiated to reduce the structure weight and armament was reduced to four cannon.

The three-view drawing of the XP-62, below, shows that the design had retained nothing of the P-40, its illustrious ancestor. Difficulties with the pressure cabin brought an early demise to the programme.

(Above and below) Two views of the sole prototype of the Curtiss XP-62, the last piston-engined fighter designed for the USAAF by the company.

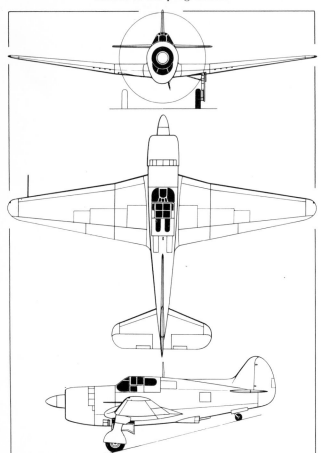

A letter contract for 100 P-62s was approved on 25 May 1942 but two months later it was cancelled to allow Curtiss to concentrate upon production of the P-47G Thunderbolt. The first XP-62 was completed in time for a first flight to be made on 21 July 1943, but without the cabin pressurization equipment — for which the York Ice Machinery Co was responsible — and although the aircraft was kept in flight status for a few months in the hope that the equipment could be installed and tested, it never was, and no flying took place after August 1944. Work on the XP-62A had been cancelled in September 1943.

Curtiss XP-62 Specification
Power Plant: One Wright R-3350-17 air-cooled 18-cylinder two-row radial engine with turbo-supercharger, rated at 2,300 hp for take-off and 2,250 hp in military rating at 25,000 ft (7 625 m). Curtiss Electric six-blade contra-prop, diameter 13 ft 2 in (4,02 m). Max fuel, 384 US gal (1 453 l).
Performance: Max speed, 448 mph (721 km/h) at 27,000 ft (8 235 m), 358 mph (576 km/h) at 5,000 ft (1 525 m); time to climb to 15,000 ft (4 575 m), 6.59 min; service ceiling, 35,700 ft (10 890 m); take-off distance to 50 ft (15,2 m), 2,350 ft (717 m); landing distance from 50 ft (15,2 m), 2,140 ft (653 m); endurance, 1.5 hrs with max fuel.
Weights: Empty, 11,773 lb (5 345 kg); design gross, 14,-660 lb (6 656 kg); max take-off (full fuel), 16,651 lb (7 560 kg).
Dimensions: Span, 53 ft 7¾ in (16,35 m); length 39 ft 6 in (12,05 m); height, 16 ft 3 in (4,04 m); wing area, 420 sq ft (39,02 m²).
Armament: Four 20-mm cannon in wings (plus optional provision for four more) with 150 rpg.